Fruit Tramps

L. H. [Luther Henry] and Linda Inez Tindal, 1979

Herman LeRoy Emmet

Fruit Tramps

A Family of Migrant Farmworkers

Foreword by Cornell Capa

Introduction by A. D. Coleman

University of New Mexico Press

Albuquerque

Library of Congress Cataloging-in-Publication Data
Emmet, Herman LeRoy, 1943–
   Fruit tramps / Herman LeRoy Emmet.—1st ed.
      p.   cm.
   ISBN 0-8263-1119-9.—ISBN 0-8263-1157-1 (pbk.)
   1. Migrant agricultural laborers—United States.   I. Title.
HD1525.E48   1989
331.5′44′0973—dc20
89-4922
   CIP
First edition

To my adorable wife, Elaine,
for all her years of patience and support

Contents

Foreword

A coincidence has helped me write these words. We have just celebrated the golden anniversary of the publication of John Steinbeck's *The Grapes of Wrath*. The similarity between Steinbeck's Joads and the Tindals of Herman Emmet's *Fruit Tramps* is evident in this conversation between two of the protagonists of *The Grapes of Wrath:*

> "We ain't gonna die out. People is goin' on—changin' a little, maybe, but goin' right on."
>
> "How can you tell? . . . What's to keep ever'thing from stoppin'; all the folks from jus' gittin' tired an' layin' down?"
>
> . . . "Hard to say. . . . "Ever'thing we do—seems to me is aimed right at goin' on. . . . Even gettin' hungry—even bein' sick; some die, but the rest is tougher. Jus' try to live the day, jus' the day."*

Steinbeck and his book *The Grapes of Wrath* showed me the way to appreciate fully what Herman Emmet has done with his photographs. My admiration for his work soars. It is a remarkable and important story of great human value about a generational pattern of subsistence living. Emmet's compulsion to share, endure, and complete his photographic story of this family deserves kudos. It is a story I find hard to accept, but I cannot accept the fact of homelessness either.

An award to a photojournalist for being a "sharing, unflinching chronicler" could be the definition of a new trophy—one that would be very seldom given. But surely Herman Emmet has already earned that award.

Cornell Capa
Director, International Center of Photography
April 1989

*John Steinbeck, *The Grapes of Wrath* (New York: Viking Press, 1939), pp. 577–78.

Intro-duction

Trampling Down the Vineyards: Herman Emmet's Fruit Tramps

How do you tell a story that's already been told so often that no one listens to it anymore? One way is to dig down into the story, down to some deeper level of experience, emotion, and symbol—to cease merely witnessing and begin instead to bear witness to the rock-bottom truths of your tale, the things that matter, the stuff that endures.

That's not easy to do, especially not nowadays. It requires abandoning fashionable notions of contingency and relativism, turning away from the chic posture of ironic detachment. It means letting go of the prevalent conceit that you can "reinvent documentary" from SoHo lofts and the groves of academe. It involves believing in something, committing to it, and being willing to get your hands dirty with the muck of what truly concerns you.

The tale Herman Emmet tells us in *Fruit Tramps* is, on several levels, a familiar one. The best-known renditions of it are John Steinbeck's *The Grapes of Wrath* and Edward R. Murrow's "Harvest of Shame," but others (Marion Palfi, Dorothea Lange and Paul Schuster Taylor, and Paul Fusco among them) have given us classic alternate versions. Certainly no reasonably informed citizen nowadays can pretend to ignorance of the fact that fruit and vegetable pickers sit way below the salt at this culture's tables—when they're allowed into the dining hall at all.

Yet, despite such recurrent and sympathetic attention to their plight, little has changed over the past century. The migrant agricultural workers are still invisible to us. Whether treated as fictions or statistics, they themselves have remained ciphers, generic "stoop labor," flesh-and-blood servomechanisms whose existence is assumed but unquestioned. Herman Emmet's strategy here—radical in its simplicity—is to deny us the comforting insulation of that distance by plunging us abruptly and at length into the daily lives of some real people who do this work: the Tindals—L. H., Linda, Tina Michelle and Shannon—and their extended family.

The immersion is salutary, for it forces us to see them in all their fullness. The world of the Tindals, their relatives, and friends is not romanticized here. Yet despite their hand-to-mouth existence and often desperate circumstances, these are surely not hopeless, loveless, or joyless people. Neither pathetic nor apathetic, they are instead intelligent and articulate. In fact, to a considerable extent they've chosen to live as they do, turning away from other options that offer more stability and security. What they ask for is not revolution, merely reapportionment—the right to a share of the profits from their labor, a share just large enough to enable them to live decent working-class lives.

Emmet's painful awareness of the marginality of the Tindals' situation does not blind him to the degree to which they've determined their own destiny. Nor does that recognition convince him to ignore the flashes of magic in their daily experience—for part of what he seeks to reveal is that humans have the capacity to make the most (and sometimes, somehow, even more than that) of whatever hand is dealt to them by others or by themselves.

What Herman Emmet so obviously believes in, like L. H. and Linda Tindal, is the bedrock of family and the binding power of love. L. H. and Linda dote on their children, rely on (and are relied on by) their strongly woven network of kin and close friends, are clearly devoted to each other and maintain what seems like a remarkably egalitarian, nonsexist partnership. (Theirs is, in fact, a topsy-turvy version of that 1980s dream, the two-career marriage, with both spouses working side by side and sharing the household chores. It seems to be working better than most marriages I know.)

So there are really two stories intertwined here: a socio-political narrative of marginalization and economic exploitation, and a family chronicle of survival under duress and the surmounting of hardship. These tales do not contradict or negate each other, but they do mitigate and complexify what otherwise might be taken for granted. In short, they force us to both feel and think on two levels simultaneously. Which is exactly what Emmet had in mind.

I've known Herman Emmet since his days at the Maryland Institute, College of Art in Baltimore. He studied there with a close colleague of mine, Richard Kirstel, and was part of a graduate seminar I ran as a visiting lecturer. That seems an age ago. Now he's a mature, full-fledged working photographer who's produced an important piece of work. *Fruit Tramps* is a serious exploration of a significant subculture within the rapidly growing North American underclass; at the same time, it is also a powerful firsthand account of some exemplary lives lived in that milieu.

I've followed Emmet's work on this project from its early phases on. He subjected this testament to an elaborate critical/self-critical process during the years of its making. The end result is a first-rate example of social-documentary photography, in the tradition of the Walker Evans–James Agee collaboration, *Let Us Now Praise Famous Men.*

Emmet's photographic style is, of course, different from Evans's: the intimacy, informality, and fluidity the small camera makes possible are evident here. The photographs are rich in information—about gesture, body language, facial expression, interpersonal relations, environment. Yet they're unforced, unposed, and alive with feeling; it's as if the viewer were privileged to look over the shoulder of someone who's a member of this crowd.

To some extent, this is because Emmet has cultivated a kind of unobtrusiveness that the best documentary photographers achieve. But in large part this is due to Emmet's having photographed not as an outsider but from the participants' perspective, seeing and describing their world from the vantage point of one who, though not from their world, has worked, sweated, eaten, and slept alongside them.

The world of the Tindals appears here as a microcosm, a self-contained universe. Except by implication, as in the images made at the supermarket and in the dentist's office, there's no one present but family and friends. According to the photographer, this isolation accurately reflects the segregation (some of it self-imposed) that separates fruit tramps from the larger society. Emmet has deliberately restricted his cast of characters, sacrificing breadth for depth. The breadth—general pictorial surveys of the migrant condition—can in any case be found elsewhere. But the depth (including the extended chronological frame, almost a decade) is unprecedented.

As a result, the complexity and richness of the Tindals' situation can unfold itself, all in good time. Their lives are shown as immersed in the physical world—dependent on their own bodies and wits for day-to-day survival in a struggle for the basics: food, shelter, clothing, medical care, transportation. The toll that this hardscrabble existence takes on them—exhaustion, premature aging, recurrent illness, and major dental problems—is visible in Emmet's images, and carefully observed.

All the same, and due perhaps to that very physicality, they seem to inhabit their world fully, adults no less than children. They take pride in their work, pleasure in their play, joy in each other, and they let it show. From the pictures, one can see something of what attracts the Tindals to the picker's life, what binds them so tightly to their own condition. One can also sense how even this nomadic, uncertain life could be an extraordinary adventure to children who know they're deeply loved.

Emmet is not so seduced by the Tindals' vitality that he loses his critical distance. The irony of the photo that shows L. H. stepping out at night from the decrepit shell of a Future Farmers of America tour bus to take a leak is deliberate and sharp. Yet he is not so appalled by their problems that he fails to notice their vitality, their affection, their general competence at making do. Such qualities are not easily revealed by photographs; it's a tribute to Emmet's commitment to the Tindals, and their consequent trust of him, that they disclose themselves to us so un-self-consciously through his lens.

What is most surprising about the Tindals, at least to me, is their thoughtful awareness not only of their own lives and choices but of the larger political context that to a considerable extent determines their condition. This understanding is not within photography's power to make manifest, but it is central to Emmet's purpose, which is to show these people as neither dry instances nor broken victims but, instead, as fully human beings.

For that reason, his description of them is not only imagistic but textual. I think it's important to note that Emmet considers this book, as a whole, to be (as he says, quietly and in passing, in his preface) "a work of literature." Though that is still not a claim we're accustomed to hearing for a book so involved with photographs, there are certainly precedents for it—in addition to the Agee–Evans collaboration, we have the image-text works of the team of Margaret Bourke-White and Erskine Caldwell, Wright Morris, and quite a few others. It strikes me as a reasonable assertion in this case, for Emmet is surely a storyteller.

He lays no claim to being a major stylist; his is a blunt, clean prose, spare as the lean lives he describes. Unlike Agee's, his writing is only rarely poeticized; but it has the resonance and authority of experience in its tones. The language of his characters is rendered straightforwardly; Emmet's own accounts and observations are thoughtful, understated, yet clearly grounded not only in research but in his own time spent living with his protagonists.

Of this involvement Emmet says, "The major issues of migrant life—such as its effect on the lives of children—do not reveal themselves quickly. You need more material to tell the full story. So I had to learn to see this as a long-term project, like what I imagine to be the process of sitting down to write a novel. Hemingway," he continues, "saw his experience as a journalist as preparation for his fiction. But he knew the difference: a true narrative takes time. So this isn't photojournalism in the usual sense; I watched myself cross over into something that I have no other word for but literature."

The resonant tone of this book as a whole is a result of that "crossing over," Emmet's decision to commit himself to his sense of the story's internal time frame. It creates a context of credibility, giving his version of this North American saga a weight and value it could otherwise not achieve. And I think the images and text are of a piece, integral—that, in mood, tone, and awareness they complement and enhance each other, living up to L. H.'s requirement that the tale be told "true blue."

In my opinion, this book serves its subjects well. I'm speaking of both its subjects: the specific people whose lives it describes, and the migrant-labor caste they represent. The individuals are served by being treated as such; they are given their own names and voices, the chance to tell their stories and make their case, the opportunity to present themselves to a culture that chooses not to see them. The caste of which they're part (and the snarl of issues implicated in that caste's situation) is served through Emmet's persistent integration of the particular and the general—his subtle but determined contextualizing of one family's story within a broader social/political/economic frame, and his simultaneous insistence that the overview not neglect the specific human consequence of institutional forces.

I also think the project serves the medium of photography, as an unpretentious, nonbravura reminder of what serious, prolonged inquiry can achieve within a traditional form when undertaken by someone devoted enough to the subject to learn it from the inside out before picking up the camera. Obviously, it helps to have that be someone unconcerned with aesthetic fashion, who recognizes the limitations of photographs and the utility of words, and is not afraid to function as a storyteller.

Herman Emmet's models, I know, are Agee–Evans and W. Eugene Smith, among others. This work emerges from that lineage, extends the thrust of those seminal efforts, and deserves to stand in their company. But it certainly is not of interest exclusively to those concerned with serious photography, who may well prove to be only a small segment of its audience. Like the best work of those people I've just named, *Fruit Tramps* is a substantial and deeply moving statement that I suspect will be found valuable by people in other disciplines; I also think it may find a surprisingly sizable readership among the general public.

Indeed, if I could express a hope for this book, it would be simply that it might find its way into the hands of all who are committed to a responsible relation to those who bring to our table the food that nourishes us. If that could be managed, perhaps it would bring us, like Emmet, to our feet beside the Tindals—enough of us so that at long last we might trample down the vineyards where the grapes of wrath are stored.

A. D. Coleman
Staten Island, New York
May 1989

Preface

This book is about a proud and loving family, the Tindals. It is not a book about poverty, nor politics, nor is it a textbook about the general world of migrant farmworkers. It is a chronicle in both images and words of the time I spent with the Tindals, extremely articulate people, acutely aware of the political, social, and economic facts of life. A white, indigent migrant family from South Carolina and Florida, they follow the seasonal harvests along the East Coast migrant stream of the United States, as far north as Lake Ontario. In earlier days, they ranged as far west as Texas and Missouri.

Over the course of seven years, I had the privilege of spending blocks of time, usually a month or so, living, eating, sleeping, working, traveling with the Tindals. I came to understand their similarities to other migrants and their uniqueness. The Tindals are similar to other migrants in that they do the same work, ride the same roads, share the vicissitudes and experiences of migrants in general. Seen in the historical context, however, they are a throwback to fifty years ago when their ethnic type, descendants of the working class of the antebellum South, fled the Dust Bowl for the valleys of Sonoma and Delano. The Tindals are the last of a breed, so to speak, a white family surrounded by migrants from other ethnic backgrounds. Today most migrants are of Latin, Asian, and Caribbean extraction.

After completing a photography document on migrant farm labor for the Lewis Hine Exhibition Committee at the Brooklyn Museum in 1977, I realized that the only way to understand the migrant in real depth would be to live and work with a migrant family. I wanted to experience the details of their daily lives in order to construct an overall picture, and to witness the effect of that life on their children. The Tindal adults, L. H. (Luther Henry) and Linda Inez (Motes), were migrants by tradition and by choice, as were their parents; they could have settled down. But the children had no choice. Malnourished and minimally educated, they tramped and picked fruit like their elders, living in tents, automobiles, and migrant labor camps.

Migrant life is not desirable, or even romantic, but it does carry on. The children will make their way by a combination of family tradition, whatever education they get, and the driving force of ambition. In a few years, Tina Michelle Tindal will come of age and be free to choose. Long ago, her older sister and brother, Tracy and Monkey, left the migrant life far behind. Will thirteen-year-old Tina, eight-year-old Shannon Dewayne, and two-year-old Nikki Nicole do likewise, or will they choose to ride the migrant road and eventually raise fourth-generation fruit tramps? That is a future story. This book is primarily a portrait of a close-knit American family living on the edge of our society, fallen through the safety net, who happen to be migrants and poor.

In 1979, with support from *Life* magazine, I began what was to become a nine-year project. Through previous contacts in North Carolina, I was able to locate a migrant family who agreed to work with me. In the past I had photographed Mexican and black American migrant farmworkers, but I felt that to understand the migrant scene with as few linguistic and racial barriers as possible, I had to find a white family, with whom I would have more in common. Experience in the field taught me that with each passing year the white migrant family was becoming more and more rare, a vanishing species. For this reason alone, it became imperative for me to photograph what I saw as the end of a line of agricultural labor, the closing of a chapter in American history.

The people at the Migrant Clinic in Hendersonville, North Carolina, knew the Tindals, and one day a nurse took me out to the family dwelling on Hogrock Road where I met L. H., Linda, and their children. They thought I was a doctor because I had arrived with a nurse from the clinic. When I explained who I was, why I was there, and the nature of my project, they were surprised, very surprised that I would want to do a story about them. I said I would come back in a couple of days, during which time I would appreciate their considering my idea.

When I returned, the Tindals agreed to the proposal, but only on the condition that I work with them in the fields and be able to tell the story "true blue," as L. H. put it. He, Linda, and other farmworkers had seen occasional spot-journalistic pieces on migrants and they deemed such stories inadequate. They felt they would like someone to document migrant life more fully and tell a tale to the outside world from firsthand experience so that they, migrants, might be perceived as human and significant.

With migrant farmwork, all the variables of the long haul over many years of migrant existence must be taken into consideration for a true life-style picture to emerge. Migrant life is measured not in days, but in the cycles of endless seasons, and in the decades of the rising at dawn and the resting at dusk of an invisible people. The who, what, where, when, and how of migrant life can be answered by journalism, but not the why. That is the task of a work of literature, such as this, a distillation of life as it was actually lived, a slow passage of time necessary for impressions and details to sink in. If that life is convincing to the reader, then the why will emerge, along with the truth.

The text is drawn from notebooks kept during my stays with the Tindals. So many things were new to me that I wrote them down almost daily, in huge spurts, usually at night when the family was asleep, because I knew I would never remember quotidian details with clarity as time went by. The text includes transcripts* from audio and video tapes done with the full knowledge and approval of the family members.

It also contains paraphrased and condensed versions of conversations I had with the Tindals—repeated conversations on the basic themes of migrant life. We talked in cars, around campfires, or during lunch breaks while picking fruit. Sometimes I would ask a question about a detail of fruit-tramp life; sometimes the Tindals wanted to speak their minds to me so that I could better understand them and their world.

*Some of the Tindals' frank opinions spring from resentment produced by harsh economic and immigrant pressures, not from racial prejudice.

Acknowl-
edgments

Acknowledgments and thanks, alphabetically, to:

Margaret V. F. Belknap, for her unquestioning support.

Allan (A. D.) Coleman, for his critical assistance.

Barbara, Bill, and 'Dearie' Garrison, for all their help.

Frank Grant, for his introduction to the world of farmworkers.

John Loengard, for his project support during his tenure as photo editor at *Life*.

John Szarkowski, for his recognition and the confidence which that inspired.

Luther Wilson, for his love of photography.

Fruit Tramps

Gesture

Radio static and the country wail of southern crooners drifted through the house while the Tindals lay sleeping. Johnny Cash sang "Ghost Riders in the Sky," occasionally off tune. Honky-tonk wafted softly all night from their room between the cracklings of summer lightning in the North Carolina mountains.

Three-year-old Tina Michelle Tindal cried out, "Momma!" Reaching down with a muscular arm, her father, L. H., picked Tina up from her mattress on the floor and put her between himself and Linda on their rickety pink-paint-flecked bronze bed. Rain thundered down on the sheet-metal roof.

I lay awake in the next room. Musty smells from my ancient, creaky cot and the sounds of a dripping kitchen spigot were new to me. Restless, I stepped outside. A full moon shimmered off the water. A gentle wind moved down the canyon, and the creek behind the shack made liquid sounds. Above, on the ridge, a wild dog barked, and the echo reverberated into silence. Toads croaked in tandem, a solitary owl hooted, and trees were silhouetted against the stars. I turned in.

Radio announcements about the price of hog feed and fertilizer woke us at 5 A.M. Linda came in to set the coffee water boiling and bacon ends on the woodstove fire. I rose from my bunk and sat down at the wooden table across the room next to the potbellied stove. She asked how I took it. I said with milk and a little sugar. L. H. came in and slid into a chair as if in a dream. Taking some steamy grits with a crooked aluminum fork and a push of Wonder Bread, he handed me ten dollars. The grower had paid our piecework, and now L. H. was giving me my share. I told him to keep it. He held the bill for a moment, then folded it into his left shirt pocket in a gesture so supple and complete that you could have missed it.

I saw that deft arm movement repeated many times during our time together, because that's the pocket where he stashed his money, and that's the hand that threw those devastating pinochle tens and trumps, and snatched citrus from trees across the continent. Over the years, that hand, wrist, and arm had developed a style as fluid as a quarterback's.

L. H. and Linda knew I knew they had no money to speak of.

Most of it had bought eggs, grits, beer, and cigarettes. Now it was gone, and the point about being poor and broke is that it makes you get up at dawn. You have to, to survive. That day, we'd have to start slinging squash into bins at dawn and work until sundown to earn another ten dollars each.

(1979)

Monkey

Morning mist clung to the squash field in long layers, drenching the trousers of the fruit tramps working fast and quietly in the semidarkness. The hazy red August sun rose hot and humid on their backs.

They tossed big pumpkin-sized squash one by one down the line to large wooden bins. An orange squash burst on impact, spilling potential Gerber baby food out through the slats. It didn't matter. This was a bumper crop, and there was plenty for Gerber.

We smashed and broke the thorny, thick vines with our fists and feet. We tore the heavy squash up and threw it into bins in one conveyed thrust.

You had to keep up and go fast because the quicker you picked the more bins you made, and you got paid by the bin. Nobody liked a slacker, because he'd get an equal cut. If he didn't shape up, no one would work with him, and he'd get frozen out.

Talk was not idle, because no one had the strength to run his mouth for no reason. In the heat of midday, the boss man came out with a free, on-the-house soda pop break, and scanned our work. He said we were doing real fine, and hoped to see us tomorrow, "so that we can finish off them two blocks up yonder behint them trees."

Then we got back to work. I heard Monkey go down: thud, tripped, boot caught on a vine, smashing his head on a boulder as big as the squash he'd been toting. His father picked him up off the ground and away from snakes. Blood drenched his forehead, and L. H. took his own shirt off and held it to the gash. He turned and asked me to take Monkey (Luther, Jr.), a son by his first wife, to the Hendersonville (N.C.) Migrant Clinic.

Ten-year-old Monkey gripped my hand as we trampled through the tall, weedy plants past other tramp pickers to the edge of the field and the tar country road. He held his father's shirt to his head, staring straight ahead as he strode.

Mute, as if in shock, he tried to hide his true feelings, tried to be a man. But I knew he was in pain. He had to be, with a wound that big and nasty.

Dark blood ran down his neck, over his collar bone, and across the crusts of sweat and dirt on his chest. He began to cry.

(1979)

Bamboo Cane

Mexicans arrived wearing long hair, a few with bandannas around their heads, talking in low voices. They leaned against a wall in a line, arms crossed, and one booted foot to the wall, like sleeping cranes. Ones with hats pulled the wide cane brims down over their eyes against the low angle of the sun.

Like the Tindals, they had worked their way through Georgia for peaches and South Carolina for squash. Momentarily they were here in North Carolina for beans and apples. But come late October, early November, with the mountains windy and cold and the harvests complete, they head back to mine the Florida Gold out of citrus farms as big as Luxembourg.

A crew-leader bus drove up the 7th Avenue depot and the migrants got on. It rolled away out to the orchards, and we followed behind in the Tindals' beat-up Barracuda, squeaking and clanking through the cool morning and back country roads of Hendersonville.

We pushed our way through some apple trees' short cut to a broad opening under the sky. There, lit in slanted rays, stretched a lush green bean field. The pickers quickly chose their individual rows and got down on their knees, tossing beans into tall wooden baskets, leaving stripped vines behind.

Veteran migrants, too stiff from years of labor to stoop or squat or kneel in the rich black soil, sat on stools and wooden crates they'd brought to the job, and picked by reaching down. A grandfather, black in worn gray flannels and elastic blue suspenders, leaned on a rickety bamboo cane as he hobbled, pulling his bushel of bunch beans behind. His bright pink shirt glowed and fluttered in the heat above the green horizon, like a flag.

The youngest of the workers, Tina Tindal, collected her beans in a plastic quart container her dad had cut open. Four years old, Tina Michelle wanted to do what the grown-ups were doing, and broke out in tears when she couldn't have a big bushel basket like theirs. So they let her carry the next empty down the row to where they could load it, and that stopped her crying.

In actual fact, it was the extreme heat and blinding sun that had driven Tina Michelle to tears. No food had passed her lips that day. No money had come to L. H. and Linda for food, as no work had been available. The month-long rains had wasted the prime produce fields. Only scraggly bunch beans remained, and few of them at that. This was "survival pickin'," as L. H. called it, something the Tindals tried to stay away from because they couldn't make any real money off it. It would help them survive 'til the apples came in. There was better and sometimes real money in picking fruit, while it lasted. Today, the Tindal family made twenty dollars among the five of them, with Tina and Monkey contributing what they could.

(1979)

Hole in
the Wall

L. H. sat on the side of the bed sipping coffee from a white ceramic cup with a broken handle. The door was open to the chilly dawn air. He had on his torn dungarees, no shirt, and bare feet. A small feeble bulb in the ceiling of the room flickered on the mountain fog.

In the dim light, you could barely see that his left foot had four toes; the small one had been blown off by gunshot. He was missing half his right heel; a bullet had gone through that and had left a hole that just about passed daylight. Like a James Dean epitaph, tattoos read on his right shoulder, "live hard," on his chest, "love fast," and on his left shoulder, "die young."

"Heard you comin'," he said. I had driven up the mountain, breaking the predawn silence, shifting gears around the hairpins of Hogrock Road. He lit a cigarette and scratched his head. Linda lay asleep with Tina at her side. It was at this time of day, before sun-up and work, that L. H. and I would talk to each other in low voices.

We talked about our chances of finding work, who was picking what where, and hoped we didn't have to drive too far to find it. A long commute meant time out of the fields and considerable gas money, a big bite out of profits.

Linda awoke depressed and weary, and not feeling well. Jim, an old fruit tramp friend who was staying with them a few days, offered to take her to the clinic in his car. She turned him down, knowing she had to go to work with the rest of us.

L. H., Linda, and I drove over to visit a friend of theirs, Billy, not far from where we hoped to do early apples. On the way, we swung by and got Calvin, an older brother of L. H.'s. He stumbled out of his antique trailer, bleary-eyed and hung over. Calvin says he has tried to stop drinking but can't. Says he's too old to learn new tricks. One day he won't wake up, remarks Linda.

At Billy's, we passed around Calvin's bottle of vodka. Its warmth felt good, and I settled back on the couch next to Billy's wife, Barbara, who was curled up under a blanket. The tarpaper cabin was as unpretentious as its inhabitants, who were enjoying a kind of family roughhouse.

Billy handed me a framed picture of his beautiful seventeen-year-old daughter, Tanilla, saying that she looked just like her photo. With a smile, he yelled out to her to get her "lazy butt" out of bed. She shouted back, jokingly, that he could "just kiss my ass."

She ducked under the covers and screamed as he pushed in her door. Barbara cried out, "Give her seventeen licks for me," while he feigned spanking her backside. When he returned, everybody was laughing.

She sure was a beauty. She came into the room wearing tattered short shorts and a brief tee shirt and yawned, stretching her long full body against the flimsy tight fabric. L. H. looked at me, winked, and rolled his eyes. Tanilla was the one he had a date with, or so he said. Linda didn't say much; she knew L. H. was a lot more talk than action. Generally, he kept his hands to himself and was a loving family man.

There was a view of the rolling, highland valley through the kitchen window frame, a hole in the wall with no pane, as if the carpenter had run out of materials. The sun shone on orchards of deep green apple trees undulating in the Appalachian distance. They were owned by others, cousins and distant kin, our employers. There wasn't anything growing in these parts that wasn't owned by a relative or acquaintance of somebody.

Cool October air blew through the hole in the kitchen wall. As we all stood up to leave and make for the door, the empty bottle of vodka whistled through the hole and crashed in the valley below. It was time to go to work.

(1979)

Ancestors

L. H.'s father was a sharecropper in South Carolina. As such, he received a share of the profits from the landowner's crops. But working another man's land didn't pay. "I left the farm, hit the road, and became a migrant," he said just before he died in 1979 at sixty-eight, a ripe age for a migrant.*

My daddy was one hell of a man, reflected L. H. almost ten years later, in May 1988. *I ain't half the man he was. I never could fill his shoes.*

Before he turned to sharecropping, Woodrow Tindal did, at one time, own his own land, but L. H. does not know what became of it. Linda's mother and father picked fruit for a living in Florida, and their family is also tied to agriculture.

L. H. and Linda are now at least the fourth generation of Tindals to live off the land. The family history includes bootlegging, shotgun deaths over Carolina swamp moonshine stills, and doing time in a southern penitentiary.

Of their grandparents, beyond the fact of Cherokee blood, what they know is sketchy. George Tindal, L. H.'s grandfather, owned land and cotton in Pelion, South Carolina. Linda's paternal grandfather, James Elihu Motes, farmed and raised cotton in Mississippi and Missouri; on her mother's side, Grandpa Goff farmed in Arkansas.

L. H.'s maternal grandfather, Sonny Hoover, a full Cherokee Indian from North Carolina, picked cotton and worked slaves in South Carolina. A grown man, he married L. H.'s grandmother, Lue Blackville, when she was 16, had a son named Jude, and, L. H. recollects, a brother named Hamp. Sonny was "older than kerosene"; as he lived to be 109, and died in the 1950s.

I hate what the white man done to the Indians. My granddaddy, Sonny Hoover, full-blooded Cherokee, owned the whole

---

*It is generally felt, though not proved (according to the U.S. Public Health Service), that the average farmworker dies far sooner than the average American, who lives to be seventy-two.

*of Lexington County at one time. The white man took it away
from him.*

About most of their early ancestors, their names and origins
and where they first settled in the South, they know little or nothing,
though the Tindals have inhabited South Carolina for two hundred
years.

(1979)

Broken Your Butt

The mountains blurred black on the faint sky of Edneyville, N.C., as I steered down the long twisty macadam. Turned right on Hogrock, and my lights picked out in detail the rocks and furrows of the dirt road as it led up and up, bend after bend, to the Tindals'. Almost missed the slip of their side feeder as it's concealed by bramble. You turn right, over a bump and fallen dogwood branches, and shoot obliquely down to their green shack lying in a hollow. It's so quiet you can tell who's going by from the sound of the truck. People mostly drive pick-ups in this area.

Hogrock bends up and around to the left of the hollow past the landlord's fruit trees. He lives higher up the mountain, and lets the Tindals stay in their shack as long as they'll pick for him the moment his fruit comes in, which it hadn't yet. We were free-lancing around the area working for other people while the landlord's fruit got some size. But the results of the free-lancing were hit or miss. We couldn't wait 'til it came in.

Picked up L. H. and Calvin and went over to Five Corners in Dana where we waited for a grower to arrive. Never did. Who knows why? We tried someplace else. Nothing. We knew the different growers and were trying to meet them at various places, but our luck was bad. Then we struck paydirt.

On Route 64 going down toward Chimney Rock, we stopped at a small orchard packing house. Nobody. We were either too early in the morning or the apples weren't ready. But just then an old farm truck piled high with apple boxes zoomed by, followed by two cars brimming with pickers. I said to L. H. and Calvin that maybe we should tag along. L. H. said, "Hell, why not? We ain't got nothing to lose."

Well, about twenty miles later, 'way past Lake Lure, we all stopped at a store for lunch provisions. As I pulled up to the truck, L. H. leaned out the window and asked the driver, "Do you need any help?" The grower answered, "Can you pick apples?" "Yep," we all piped up from inside the car. "Well, O.K., just follow me." And we did for another ten miles, without the slightest idea where we were heading, but it didn't much matter. We all wanted to work, and had to work.

We ended way up in the hills somewhere near Springs, N.C.,

a place not even on the map. By the time we got our pick sacks and ladders from the boss man and were walking out to the trees, it was already 10 A.M.

It was slow, hot work, and I believe it was a psychological drag to have arrived so late in the morning. It made the work tedious and the time tick slowly by. On an average day, you get out there just as the sun's coming over the hills and have the advantage on the time and heat. By 2 P.M., you've already picked a whole bunch of bins and know that there are only a few more to go. By 4 or 5 in the afternoon, when the hot, blazing heat's just about killed you, you pack it up, return the pick sacks, get your piece-rate money from the boss, and head on home. In spite of the physical duress, there's definitely some kind of pride and dignity in this labor—you've broken your butt, your body aches from the sweat and toil, but you feel good about it.

Nobody spoke and nobody took a lunch break. We grabbed the apples off the trees straight through to 5 P.M. closing time, last chance to get paid by the grower, and finished up with ten bins (crates). At $7.50 each, we made $25 per person, roughly $4.15 an hour. Besides beginning late, we had little Tina Michelle in the orchards with us today. Every now and then she'd cry out for her mommy or daddy, who'd have to come all the way down the ladder. Well, that was a pick sack right there, maybe a hundred apples, they'd lose having to tend to her. She'd feel lonely; everyone'd be toiling away and she'd be playing by herself and get bored or into trouble, like getting stung or disappearing out of sight or getting in the way of the fork lift. In Florida, they use a thing called a "goat," a type of vehicle that lifts up your full bin of oranges and dumps them into a container on the back. It looks like a scorpion with its long-armed pincer stretching to the rear.

Usually, Tina goes to a wonderful day-care center for migrant children in East Flat Rock, near Hendersonville. They pick her and the other kids up in a school bus early, take them from migrant camp, trailer, or shack to the center, then feed them, nap them, bathe them if they need a bath, teach the ABC's, numbers, personal hygiene. The children watch instructional movies, finger paint, and play with blocks and toys of every description, generally getting things their home environments don't offer.

This day care is only one example of the fine support provided by the greater community of Hendersonville, North Carolina, to both seasonal and migrant farmworkers. The area is highly agricultural and requires a dependable source of migrant labor each year. The community welcomes the pickers by providing primary health care and hospital services, food, housing, employment, and economic benefits, as well as a host of other programs funded through state and federal allocations of money and run by the local community. The Migrant Council, Inc., of Hendersonville takes a special interest in providing these migrant programs and makes sure they actually work.

The Tindals, among other migrants, are aware of these services and are thankful they exist. They say other places they go to in the Southeast, including the big agricultural areas of Florida, never have what Hendersonville has. They say the services simply don't exist. If you listen to a lot of migrants, which is the one quick way to find out who's got the programs, you discover that North Carolina is the only state in the region to offer such a wide range.

(1979)

Car Swap

Linda and L. H. finally got rid of their Barracuda they'd driven many a mile. L. H. said it had about 150,000 miles on it, and he might not have been exaggerating.

He decided to swap the Barracuda and forty dollars for a junkyard '62 Chevy, whose engine ran with a perceptible knock but whose history L. H. knew as it had once belonged to one of his brothers. The brother himself had swapped it one season for something to barge him and his family through the orchards.

Well, the Chevy's no prize, but it'll go from here and back, though it's got no accelerator pedal, and the original floorboards have been replaced by sheetmetal and screws. The tinny radio plays static over voice, and the tires are paper thin.

The old Barracuda wobbled in the left front wheel when I first met the Tindals, and one of the back doors closed like an opened sardine can. It really did look and sound like a car running 1936 Okie migrants to California.

All around, the Chevy's in better condition, giving the Tindals more reliable transport to the orchards, some of which are miles away. This raised everyone's spirits. Tina Michelle got up on the hood and danced around. She felt happy because her daddy and mommy were happy, and for the moment their problems were solved. We took off from a junkyard filled with cars, guarded by mongrels straining on rusty chains. We loped down the tree-and-kudzu-ivy-lined country road to dusk and to the chance of apples at dawn on Sugarloaf Mountain.

(1979)

X-Ray Vision

Last night we played five card draw. The stakes went up and up, from a quarter a bet to two dollars toward the end. By that time everybody was pretty much liquored up and smoked out so that the game went crazy, with L. H. about falling off his chair from wild excitement, laughing and swigging vodka from a bottle that went round and round the wooden table.

Tracy, L. H.'s daughter by his first wife, hung on to her daddy's arm as he played, and little Tina slept soundly under a blanket on the sagging, sandy-colored couch right through the din of the smokey card game. She was used to her family's nocturnal activities, though most nights she and her elders were asleep by ten after the labor of harvest that day, and in preparation for the day to come at dawn.

Tonight was a happy time. Their old buddy, Jim, had come across the mountains from Tennessee on his way to see a young lady in Spartanburg, South Carolina, and had poked around the hills of Hendersonville, Dana, and finally Edneyville, before he found his friends, the Tindals, in their two-room shack off Hogrock Road up toward Sugarloaf Mountain. He had located them through the time-tested method of asking the locals, some of the growers the Tindals had picked for in the past, as well as some people who had sold them food and cashed their apple checks.

They invited Jim, now a divorced bachelor, to eat and spend the night, or to stay with them as long as he wanted. It so often went like this: old friends, kin, errant brothers, ex-con acquaintances, drifters like Dave the half-crazed ex-Marine, half-brilliant 'Nam vet—all nomadic Southerners bearing fealty to the Tindals as a tribal core. They came and went in the Tindals' life. And as many times as I was with the Tindals, and as little as they had to offer, I never once saw them turn away a friend nor fail to extend the hand of generosity. The unwritten law of the tribe held that what went down went around.

I had a ten-dollar bill I was winning and losing. There weren't enough one-dollar bills for change, so whoever had the ten had to bet it down on the ante or give it up when they lost. Once, Jim had such a fine hand that he bet fifty dollars, and we all just about dropped dead. Of course, he was kidding, but he did lay down a beautiful straight flush, and picked up the ten.

I got it back in a couple of hands, and L. H. managed to hold onto it for a while though he was drunk as a skunk. Linda was only slightly more sober and hence occasionally had the edge over L. H. and Jim, who were decidedly more experienced at poker but less sober. Of the four, I was definitely the newcomer, outfoxed and, plied with generous amounts of vodka, destined to lose my hard-earned fruit-tramp ten-dollar bill.

Old X-ray vision, that's what we called Jim. He picked up the bill on the last round as he laid down two pairs of tens, with an ace of spades in the hole. Linda dropped the cigarette from her mouth as her jaw just about hit the table. Leaning forward across the table to get a good look at Jim's hand, L. H. slipped off his chair onto the floor. The full Bud he was holding broke loose from his hand, flew up in the air spewing beer in every direction, hit the edge of the table, and tumbled upside-down into my lap, foaming.

The card game dissolved into loud laughter and heated, but friendly, accusations of cheating. L. H. cracked the seal on another quart of vodka, and passed it round. As it came my way, I sensed a certain disequilibrium. I tipped the bottle back and saw the room spinning. The last thing I remember was handing the bottle to Linda who, the next morning, recalled how I had passed out on the table with my face in my cards.

(1979)

Stumps

Luther Henry got all his teeth pulled today. Linda lost five with four left. L. H. lost fifteen with none left. He's thirty-five. She's twenty-three.

The dentist pulled out the teeth one by one with large chrome forceps. Sounds of cracking bone echoed in the white, sterile room. A nurse stood by as he laid the bloody and decayed stumps on a stainless steel tray in her hand. L. H. looks much older now, with his mouth collapsed and his lips curled inward.

Luther Henry Tindal says he'll have no more dental problems or bills. He'll chew with factory-mades as he passes into middle and old age. Or he won't bother to get them at all, gumming his food like his friend James from St. Louis.

(1979)

Crossing

The Chevy's brakes gave out on dusty, gravelly Hogrock Road one morning on our way down Sugarloaf Mountain. Heading out to a full day's work in the apples at Mountain Crest, we still had to pick up some people like Calvin Tindal and James from St. Louis before getting to the orchards. The men were over at a labor camp on the other side of the mountain, but we had to get down the hairpins of Hogrock first. Rumbling around a curve, I braked, but nothing happened. The pedal went smack to the floor. I crammed the automatic transmission into low and pulled the emergency brake with both hands. Linda yelled from the back seat, "Lookey yonder! Nary a thing to do!" as she pulled the kids to her side. We were coming to an intersection, and a tractor was approaching from the right, pulling a hay wagon.

I blew the horn and flashed the lights frantically, but he kept coming. He had his hat pulled down over his eyes against the sun, and I doubt he even saw us or heard us for the noise of his green John Deere. As we shot through the crossing, bails of hay tumbled and scattered on the main road as the farmer skidded to a halt. L. H. yelled out the window, "Can't stop, ain't got no brakes!"

The road ahead started to climb, and began slowing us down. At the crest of the hill, the emergency brakes finally took hold. As they had smoked and squeaked all the way down the mountain, I'd had my doubts as to whether we'd stop at all. But the wheels came to rest, and I slammed the car into park before it had a chance to roll back.

L. H. jumped out, popped the hood open with a blow of his fist, and poured the rest of his beer into the master brake cylinder reservoir. "Now, pump it," he said. I worked the pedal, pushing the beer down the brake lines, and got my pressure back. I put the car in drive and tested the brakes. They held.

L. H. was very proud of his cunning know-how. "I bet you never saw that done before," he said, tipping back a new beer. "Bet you never learned that in college."

(1981)

'glades

Armadillos shot from the garbage pile past our feet. Headlights lit the night marauders and sent them scooting. Their eyes glowed like small silver moons dancing in the dark.

We'd been tearing up the countryside of Loxahatchee, Florida, gathering firewood we'd hauled to the camp on the hood of the battered Dodge Dart. Calvin, L. H., Ray, and I took and piled up the huge faggots, threw on raw gasoline, and struck a match.

A giant fireball rolled toward us like an ocean wave, lit our campsite, our oily, dusty faces, and our rumpled clothes. We looked like escapees, perched on the edge of the Everglades.

At night, wild creatures emerged. Once, camping about fifty feet from the Tindals, I woke up to the sounds of an animal sniffing at my tent. I snuck through the flap and, just around the corner, switched on a flashlight.

Two eyes moved back. I couldn't make out the predator for the brush. They were big and yellow, not close together like a dog's, but wide apart, like a large cat's. Calvin snored under a tree. It had gone right past him.

Next morning, I told him what I'd seen. I figured he'd know something about it. Calvin lived out in the bush weeks at a time and slept under the stars. He opined it was a rare Everglades panther, one of a few left, and that back in the old days, you used to see a lot more of them. "But they still come 'round," he said. "You see 'em at twilight. They're real beautiful critters."

In a deep, slow Southern drawl pushed out through his large tangled moustache, Calvin swore to me on a invisible stack of Bibles that twelve-foot alligators roamed in the irrigation canal system, and could be mean. "Out in the 'glades, you can swim with 'em and they won't do you no harm," he said.

"But here," he pointed, "the gators feel threatened. They get mean 'cause of all the diggin' and plantin', you know, 'cause of all the new groves and airports and housin' that are takin' the 'glades away from the animals, includin' the panthers. One day, it'll all come to an end.

"Sometimes I see the 'gators sunnin' on the canal banks while

I'm pickin' fruit. You get to know 'em after a while. People think there's nary a difference 'tween 'em. But I can tell which is which. Each one is different."

(1981)

One Percent Right

The irrigation canal stretched straight as a ruler for miles down through the citrus, bringing water in from the Everglades. Tina Michelle skipped along the top of the levee to a point where the water deepened and looked cleaner. Linda followed, hugging her baby son, Shannon Dewayne, to her hip with that very maternal sway, and every so often would pause and peer down into the canal. Stopping at Tina's spot, she sat down on the bank, laying Shannon in her lap, and looked up and down the canal for alligators.

She told Tina to run back and fetch a towel, took her son's diaper off, slid down the embankment, and lowered him into the water. As she lathered him up, he cried and reached out to her to end this chilling bath. Waiting for the right moment, Tina handed her the towel.

Later in the day, Linda came down to the canal to wash her hair. It was not easy for her to find a clean spot in the water; an oily residue covered the surface, possibly run-off from spraying the fruit. She poked around with her hand, making a hole in the thick scum, bent over, lowering her hair into the water, and massaged shampoo into her hair. Foam spread out and bubbles merged with the iridescent chemical film, reflecting its silky hues of blue-green, magenta, and purple.

Tina walked naked down to the edge, holding a small plastic basket, and bathed next to her mother. L. H. sat under an orange tree, Shannon in his lap, batting the breeze with brother Calvin and friend Ray.

That night, Linda made a stew with two cans of Dolores California Jack Mackerel, two cans of Thrifty Maid Spanish Style tomato sauce, rutabaga, onions, and carrots. L. H. cut open the cans with his long pocket knife, so sharpened and used that all the writing on the steel was worn away. He sawed up and down and around the tops as if through butter. Linda did the rest.

She cooked the contents in a blackened pot next to a campfire that L. H., Calvin, and Ray had built for light from wood foraged off the land. She used a small, two-burner Sears gas stove I'd brought with me. Before I'd arrived, she worked off the corner of the evening fire to cook the family meal, a long and dangerous process because of the heat and shooting sparks. She already had burns on her skin and singes and holes in her clothes. Gigantic flames threw a shower of embers overhead as we sat in the sand eating off plastic picnic plates. I looked up into the black night and saw sparks merge with the stars.

Our shadows danced in the wilderness, and I imagined predators prowling at the edge of the light. Tina Michelle grabbed a burning branch from the pyre and flew around the perimeter of the campsite like a wild fairy screaming at the top of her voice.

I had been down the road before in different places with this family knowing I could pick up and leave any time; they had to stick it out as best they could. Had no place else to go. I saw them now at their lowest ebb I'd ever seen, a moment of extreme economic deprivation and psychological numbness, living in total isolation on the rim of society, like untouchables, like outlaws with borrowed names. They had a hunted, weary look. They were not on holiday, camping out. This was not a picnic, not a movie. They had no toilet, no shower, no sink, no cradle, nothing but love. Love was their deep religion, their salvation, their sole consolation, and their children their only prize.

Linda retired Shannon Dewayne to bed in the tent, came back out, and sat down with the rest of us.

L. H.: I'm thinkin' seriously about making this the last trip on the road, settle down, get me, the old lady, and the kids a home, and just, the hell with this travelin'.

Herman: Carolina?

L. H.: Definitely. It would have to be Carolina.

Linda: The onliest place fittin' to live is Carolina.

Herman: How 'bout Florida?

Linda: You call this livin', this god-forsaken sandpile where growers make you live like this, like animals in the woods? 'least in Carolina they got places you and your younguns can stay at while you pick for 'em. That ain't askin' too much.

L. H.: Hey, Herman, you wanna know what runs this state? Citrus and cocaine. No, my preference is definitely Carolina.

Linda: I love North Carolina.

L. H.: I just like the mountains. I like the mountain air, and I like the mountain people.

Linda: I like South Carolina, too. But I like North Carolina better, up in them mountains, I do. I love the view of them mountains.

L. H.: That's what I'm thinkin' of definitely doing, is hangin' it up there, just say the hell with it, just get me a steady job.

Ray: Well, that's what you feel like, but you won't. Believe me, L. H.

L. H.: Oh, I can do it. I know I can do it.

Ray: L. H.? That's what you feel like, but once you get away from it, you always come back.

L. H.: I don't know. I've been away from it before and I've . . .

Herman: Is that what happened to you, Ray, you got away from it and you came back?

Ray: Damn right.

Herman: Where did you get away to?

Ray: Vermont. West Virginia. Anywhere. I quit a job this year making ten dollars an hour just to come back pickin', and I can't make that kind of money pickin'.

L. H.: Pickin' fruit does give you a lot of freedom.

23

Linda: Yeah, Ray, we got younguns now. We got to settle down so we can keep 'em in school.

L. H.: Like you want to, you know, take a break or drink a beer? You got no time clock to punch, right?

Ray: Right! That's it.

L. H.: You got no man to answer to, except yourself and the 'goat' driver, who comes around and dumps your bins, and you ain't got to answer to him. You can pick a bin. If he fires you, hell, "pay me off," go right across the street and get another job. But it's comin' down to the point they're stoppin'. These Haitians, illegals, Mexicans, Jamaicans and all, they're takin' the jobs over, right?

Ray: Yup, that's for real.

Linda: They're takin' it all over.

Ray: They're crowdin' us out.

L. H.: No, they ain't crowdin' us out, they're just flat pushin' us out.

Calvin: I think every person in this world needs to make a livin', you know, L. H. They got a right to live, eat, just like I got a right to eat, and to live . . .

L. H.: Well, go to Haiti and make it, baby. God damn!

Ray: Calvin, do you see any of us over there takin' anythin' away from them?

L. H.: None of us.

Ray: Are we takin' *their* jobs?

Calvin: That ain't where I'm comin' from, Ray. They got a right to eat.

L. H.: Let 'em go home and eat.

Ray: Do we own [owe] 'em anythin'?

L. H.: Hell no!

Ray: Not that I know of. I'll tell you som'in, Calvin. I respect you, too. I respect where you're comin' from. But don't let 'em come in and crowd me out. I was born here.

Calvin: I . . . I think everybody has a right to eat in this world.

L. H.: Sure, I agree wid ya, everyone should have a right.

Ray: Well, we'll trade our oranges with their coconuts, or whatever, but don't let 'em come over takin' my job.

Calvin: Well, I, uh, I go along with that too, Ray. I don't like 'em pushin' me out either.

Ray: But that's what they're doin'.

Calvin: They're here, and we got to accept that.

Ray: No we don't got to. There should be someone smart enough, all of us, to do somethin' legal to get 'em out of here.

L. H.: Well, let 'em *starve!* You talk about lettin' 'em eat, Calvin. The sons of bitches lived in Haiti ten thousand years before they came over here, and they're still livin'. They got no business coming over here, and knockin' us people out of what little bit of stuff we try to earn.

Calvin: OK, I'm definitely in the wrong. OK, if that satisfies y'all, I'm in the wrong, OK? I'll go along with it.

L. H.: No, it don't satisfy me. It's . . . it's . . .

Calvin: If you can sleep better when I say I'm wrong, then I'll be wrong.

Ray: They wouldn't let us come to their country anyway, you know.

Calvin: Because they ain't got . . . you know the reason why? They ain't got no way to make a livin' over there.

Ray: We pickers over here can't even make a livin'.

Calvin: Like I say, yes sir, I'm ninety-nine percent wrong. But I'm one percent right.

Ray: I know it. You could be more right than all of us.

L. H.: Impossible. He can't be more right. He wants to take it for all them foreigners 'cause he married one of them son-of-a-bitches from over there.

Ray: Who?

L. H.: Calvin. British Honduras.

Calvin: I married strictly for money. No other reason.

Ray: Well, I don't care about that. I just care about . . .

Calvin: I'm fixin' to bug out and go to sleep because me and L. H. is going to get in an argument if I don't do it, I know that.

L. H.: No, there ain't goin' to be no argument, period.

Calvin: Yeah, but, L. H., you're so smart, and you're so right and, like I say, I'm ninety-nine percent wrong, but I do have one percent right in my body.

L. H.: Well, hell, let me ask you a question. Why do you want to take care of them?

Calvin: Because they have a right to live like I do.

L. H.: Live in their own country, not ours. They have no right in our country. We don't go to Haiti. We don't go to Cuba, we don't go to British Honduras, we don't go to Russia, It's people like you, Calvin . . .

Ray: I might be my brother's keeper, but they ain't none of my brothers. Far as I know, I ain't related to none of them.

L. H.: I tell you, if there was a drop of their blood in my body, I'd cut my damn veins and let it run out.

Ray: I stand with you on that, L. H., 'cause I do hate every damn one of them 'cause they're puttin' us short.

L. H.: I can't understand people that even likes them people from foreign countries, I tell ya. Tonight, that's my personal opinion.

Calvin: I like everybody. I don't care who he is or where he comes from.

L. H.: Well, Calvin, I got children. They takin' my job and they takin' food from my younguns.

Ray: I don't believe that I would just flat kick 'em in the face for nothin', but when they start takin' my jobs, it's time for me to look at [it] from a different direction.

L. H.: They takin' our jobs. They takin' the food from our families, and our relations, and our children.

Ray: Well, they're takin' food out of my mouth, period. That's what I care about.

L. H.: I don't really care about my . . . I can survive. I can go in a grocery store, and I can walk out with a piece of meat, or somethin', right? But my kids, man, they too young.

Calvin: L. H., listen to me closely. I got a statement to make. I don't give a hoot who you are or where you come from, he's got a right to eat, he or she.

L. H.: Go to their own country and do it. Do it in their own world, not ours. That's what I'm sayin'. Go home. Go home and do it.

Ray: Why do they want to come here for, anyway?

Calvin: There ain't much to eat over there, Ray, that's one reason.

Ray: No, they can eat good.

L. H.: They've been livin' for thousands of years without us Americans.

Calvin: But every person's got a right to have a body of food.

L. H.: They got a right to live in their own land, too. Right?

Ray: Well, I'll tell you one thing. I ain't seen too many of them come in here what was skinny.

L. H.: You're damn right. You see 'em going to work, right Ray? They got dress clothes on, fancy shoes. What do we go to work in? Nasty and filthy and dirty! The onliest things we got. But we're not recognized. They're recognized.

Ray: Who gives a damn about us? Not only me, not only you, not only Calvin, but just the people, those who, that we are. Who gives a damn?

Herman: Let me ask you, L. H. What kind of recognition would you want?

L. H.: I would like for us people, the American people, like us settin' right t'ere, American people, to be treated just half as good as them immigrants are gettin' treated.

Calvin: We are, uh . . .

L. H.: We are *not!* They are takin' it out of our pockets and puttin' it in their mouths.

Linda: They're takin' it from our younguns and puttin' it in their younguns' mouths.

(1981)

Beer Belly

We finished up early one afternoon, having done only a few bins of third-rate, lemon-sized, shriveled-up oranges that had been hit by a month-long see-saw of winter freeze and intense heat with no rain. They should have been big plump gold. No sense in working; we headed for camp.

Picked up lunch meat, bread, and cold beer at a Cumberland Farms store along Route 98 in Loxahatchee, drove west toward Belle Glade, hung a left just after an overhead flashing red light, crossed a culvert, proceeded along a narrow blacktop that became dirt after a bump where the groves began, then headed into the numberless citrus trees, and followed the trampled underbrush out to our campsite, about two or three miles off the main road.

Somewhere between our first and fourth round of sandwiches, a truck came grinding along the ruts and rocks of a grove track, heading our way. Bob the boss man pulled up, and started taking our pictures, hurriedly, from inside the cab. He did not get out.

Said he was "just taking snaps," and pointed to the Chevette. Looking over at me he asked if it was my car. I said, no, it was the Tindals'. Asked me if I had some kind of I.D. he could see, like a driver's permit. I pulled one out of my wallet, walked over and handed it up to him through the window. He did not look at me. I knew now I had become one of them, a seasonal gypsy. The man reminded me of all the people who habitually avoided direct eye contact with us as migrants. Like radar, their vision scanned the distance, warning them to stay clear, to cross to the other side of the street, as if we were diseased nomads spreading contagion, like lepers.

He passed the back of his right hand across his sweaty forehead, pulled a pencil from behind his right ear, licked it, and wrote the serial number down on a clipboard, as a policeman would do, along with my name and address. A beer can popped in the background. Vultures sheered overhead. No one spoke.

He asked if I didn't think I was a little far from home. I said, no, I didn't think so, that I was only showing him my license because I was on his property.

The man looked up in a start, his eyes bulged, and the veins on his thick neck stood out red in the glare of the sunset. Through the window he pointed a stubby finger at me, saying, "Boy, you get your smart Yankee ass outa here, and take these here people with you, and don't never come back." I thanked him for his southern hospitality. With that, he got down from the cab, and came right up. We stared at each other.

L. H. and Calvin Tindal got up and walked over swiftly. L. H. said, "Bob, your wife's likely got dinner on the table for you. Why don't you go home?" Three against one. I was ready. The man swung his heavy six-foot-three frame around, and walked his beer belly back to his truck. He paused, and stared at me for a long moment. Then he climbed in.

The truck motor broke the hot, humid silence and he tore off, swirling dust into our eyes, hair, clothes, and lunch meat. His pump shotgun hung on a rack visible through the rear window. We pulled up pegs, folded tents with the rest of our belongings into the trunk of the Chevette, and drove away, with the kids crying in the back seat that they didn't want to have to hit the road again.

The only way out to the main highway and the world beyond was by the man's house. We figured we'd head up to a campground at St. Lucie Locks, about two hours away. As his house went by, we all peered out the windows through the dry Florida dust at the imposing World War II artillery gun on the front lawn, like the kind of gun with big wheels you see at Arlington Cemetery, or on village greens in small New England towns.

Why he was throwing us out, nobody could figure. Maybe it was because he'd heard I was taking pictures, or because I'd stood up to him. Ray said, no, that Bob was just a real ornery type, and from behind his full red beard added, "He used to be a state trooper, and ain't forgot."

Ray sat in the back seat, hunched over, with his head in his hands. Linda looked at him now and then, and eventually said "What's ailin' you, Ray?"

Sitting up and leaning back into the seat, Ray remarked with a sigh that he'd had to choose between leaving with them or staying behind working full-time for Bob, whom he detested. He said he'd rather stick with his friends, but that meant he'd have to walk away from a steady job of grove work, clearing away dead trees and branches, and putting it all through a chipper to eat it up. Said he liked that better than picking fruit.

The boss man couldn't get anyone to work because he was a sonovabitch, Ray said. He went on to reveal that Bob had taken him around to some local girls just so he'd know they were available if he went to work for him. We kidded Ray that he sure had left a good thing behind. He laughed, and said, "Well, hell, them girls was so bad that even the hungry 'gators woulda turned tail an' run."

(1981)

Slam-Bam

Outsiders will use the word *migrant* or *migrant farmworker* to describe the Tindals. But once, years ago, L. H. and I happened to be waiting in the car for Linda to come out of a laundromat. We noticed three or four people walking into a Winn-Dixie supermarket next door. From the back seat where he often sat because he had no license to drive, and because Linda did the driving with no license anyway, L. H. remarked, "Yonder go tramps." Puzzled, I asked, "What do you mean by *tramps*?"

"Fruit tramps," he said, "Fruit pickers like us."

"How can you tell they're fruit tramps?" I said, wanting to get to the bottom of this name I'd never heard before.

"Field hands you can always tell. They're too broke to look any different. I could be wrong," he said, "but they sure as hell look like fruit tramps to me. It's like this, Herman, you just come out of the field, you ain't had nothin' to eat all day 'cept mebbe a sandwich an a beer, and you got some dust in your pocket from the grower, what you gonna do? You gonna go get some vittles for you and your younguns. But you ain't had time to change, and you're on your way home, and so you look like you just come out of the groves."

"But what about the word *migrant*?" I said, "Do you ever use that word?"

"Well, sometimes I do, like when I talk about migrants and the national economy, like how much we migrants contribute to the national economy, and like how much we get the short end of the stick."

L. H. dug his elbows into his sides and stretched out his hands as he continued. "All I want is a little respect for me, my family, and people like us, our kind of people. People treat us like dogs. They just want the sweat off our backs and to hell with us.

"We fill up the supermarkets of these United States every day with food, like this here Winn-Dixie. You ever go into one of them places and see all of them fat-assed people? Pathetic! They got the money to buy all that food and drive all them fancy cars. But what do we got? We got a jalopy, right? And we ain't hardly got enough money to buy grits, for chrissakes, let alone get fat. I'm skinny as a rail, my wife and kids is skinny.

"We're survivin', but it ain't easy. They treat us like dogs, like these people won't even come near us, like they cross to the other side of the street, and tell their kids not to speak to us and our kids. Why? 'Cause we look like bums.

"If the people only knew where their food came from and who put it there, that it don't grow in the supermarket, and that we contribute directly to their welfare, to their high style of living, then we might get respect. But they don't care. They don't give a damn. It just ain't fittin'.

"If all of us migrants from here to L.A. stopped pickin' for just one month, mebbe for just one day, then the American people would know who we are. All I want is a little respect for me and my family, so we can live in dignity."

"What pickers want is a decent wage," added Linda, who had returned with the clothes and was leaning through the car window from the outside. "But the farmers don't pay you nothin' you can live on. The way things are, we can barely make it, and we're out there every day fillin' them bins."

Linda paused, and L. H. was looking at her. She went on, "When it rains for weeks at a time, and there ain't no pickin' nowhere, you just gotta lay low and hope to God you don't starve, that you can get along on what little you got 'till you can get back out to the groves.

"We have busted our ass for years, but it just don't pay. We're pickers. We always have been pickers. It's in the blood. My mamma and daddy done it. L. H.'s folks's done it. All our kin done it. We've tried to get away from it, but there ain't much else we can do.

"We ain't qualified. We ain't got no schoolin' to speak of, and there ain't no real, full-time jobs out there we can do. So we always come back to the fields, and to the groves, and to hittin' the road with our younguns. It's the onliest world we know."

We were silent, and a warm puff of wind blew through the windows and rocked the car. Out in the parking lot heat waves rose off the pavement. The sky turned charcoal gray, and large drops of rain thudded on the roof while people ran holding newspapers over their heads. Linda opened the door, jumped in.

L. H. breathed in as if to collect his thoughts. "Now with all them

Jamaicans and Haitians in the field, it sure as hell don't pay. In Florida, we used to get 80 cents per box of oranges. It's now down to 40 cents. A box is about a bushel, and it takes about 10 boxes to make a bin, or a tub, like they sometimes call 'em in the groves. We used to make 8 dollars a bin, and you can pick mebbe 10 bins a day. So a man can make, if he's a good picker, and if the fruit's got some size on it, mebbe 80 dollars in a good day. Some young, fast pickers can do more than 10 bins, but not many. I've seen some of them Mexicans standing up eating lunch while they're pickin'. They really burn through them trees.

"As a family, we get up to at least 10 bins, sometimes a lot more. But now, them growers are cuttin' our wages in half, down to 40 cents a box, by bringin' in them foreigners, them contract guest workers, the Haitians and Jamaicans, and such. They'll work for half what we do, but they don't live off the economy the way we have to, and that's tough. We can't afford to work for no slave wages.

"The growers, like the ones down in Florida, like around Belle Glade, they keep them Haitians in old Air Force barracks, give 'em food, pay 'em, and then, slam-bam, ship 'em back to Haiti when they're through with 'em, when they're quit pickin'. But, now, what do they got in Belle Glade 'cause 'a them Haitians? AIDS.* That's what they got. AIDS.

"Them Haitian boat people and pickers brought it over here. And it's the growers who brought in the pickers. They shouldn't be here in the first place. They're out in the fields takin' our wages 'cause the growers won't hire us, 'cause they won't pay a decent wage so that a man, an American-born man, can feed his family and live in dignity.

"Send them slaves back to where they come from, and let us Americans have our jobs back. The growers don't care, to hell with

*"The population center with the highest per capita incidence of AIDS in the U.S. is not New York City or San Francisco, with their large homosexual communities, but Belle Glade, Fla., an isolated agricultural town of 17,000 in the center of the state. . . . The black agricultural workers live in the poor central section of town, a ghetto not only of AIDS but also of overcrowding, malnutrition, venereal disease and tuberculosis. . . . As for the global interconnection, the best guess is that AIDS began in Africa and spread to the U.S. by way of the Caribbean." *Life,* July 1985.

the poor people. That's their attitude. Herman, you been down the road with us, you know how we struggle to even survive."

Journal entry, 4/28/81: "Back in Loxahatchee, the Haitians were all over the place, and did definitely make it hard for us to find steady picking. We'd pick maybe four, five trees and run up against trees that had been picked around the sides and bottom, but not the top, by some Haitians who'd left us the hard work to do by the long ladders. If we hadn't finished up those trees, the grower would've come down our rows, seen the half-done trees, and kicked us the hell out. So we had to do 'em.

"Or we'd run into some Haitians who worked the opposite, wrong direction, and we'd have to load up the empty bins and ladders on the old Dodge and go find the man on the goat to give us a new row. Or the black guy on the goat would play favorites and not dump our bins, which meant we'd have to stop and wait for him to come around with the goat, dump the bins, punch our tickets, and then come back with empties. But he sure was dumping those Haitians' bins. He was definitely taking care of his own kind. Not much you can do about it, if you don't want to lose your job.

"Added to which we only made 40 cents a box (one pick sack, or about 175 to 200 oranges). A bin is about 10 boxes (10 pick sacks, or about 2,000 oranges), worth $4. So if you divide 2,000 into 4, you come up with the figure of .002 cent for each orange. You go to a supermarket and you'll pay a hell of a lot more than that for a orange. Someone's defnitely making a profit out of this somewhere, and it's not us. Some time ago, it used to be 80 cents a box, double a man could make, but now the growers cut that in half. Maybe 'cause of all this cheap Caribbean labor.

"From 6 A.M. to about 3 P.M. we did 9 bins and made $36. That was three of us picking, L. H., Linda, and me, picking bad trees with Haitians. It doesn't take a genius to figure out that each of us worked nine hours for $12 apiece, or $1.33 an hour. I would call this bad picking for sure. But I don't know anyone who'd work for $1.33 an hour, 'cept a migrant."

One day, picking oranges for Tropicana, we got on to *migrants* and *fruit tramps* again. I asked Linda and L. H. if they thought *fruit tramps* wasn't too negative a word.

"Hell, I fruit tramp to survive," L. H. said, "that's what I do. I like the freedom. I choose the life. *Fruit tramp* says what I am. *Migrant* don't. That's what someone else says I am. Like one 'a all dem migrants out dere. A statistic." I told them I wanted to call the book *Fruit Tramps,* and wondered if they had any objections. "Hell no," replied Linda, "that's us."

(1981)

The Old Southern Pine

We had all come back giddy from a restaurant and red wine, and the Tindals had invited me in, all of us forgetting farmer Jones's stern warning. I was back with the family again just like old times, catching up with stories, smoking and drinking, and playing pinochle, a forty-eight-card deck with two each of ace, king, queen, jack, 10, 9 in each suit, with 10 being wild.

Suddenly, a fruit tramp knocked on the door and said the farmer wanted to see me. Evidently, Jones had told someone on the property to let him know if I trespassed. I stepped outside and was met by the glare of his large, blinding flashlight. I felt glued to my tracks, rooted.

"Mista, wud I tell you 'bout keepin' offa here?" he said. With his Oldsmobile between him and me, farmer Jones stood in the driver's doorway while he leaned his right arm across the top of the car, pointing the light in my eyes. His left shoulder pitched downward as if being pulled.

In the dim light of the cloudy night, I was just able to make out his lopsided stance. I sensed he was holding something heavy in his left hand down by his side. "Now, git," he said. I knew it was no time to argue with the man, so I stepped back, got in my car, and took off, fast.

My heart pounded as I drove, not heeding where I was going but, in my adrenalized imagination, checking the rearview mirror for chase vehicles. Jones had told me the day before that if I wanted to fraternize with the Tindals, I would have to sit in my car in the country road and have them come out to visit with me. He warned me not to set foot on his property under any circumstances.

It was said that he had hung a black man from the old Southern pine that stood out near the converted pigsty, a tree as big as five trees together, with branches thick as railroad ties. I was also told that he had shot a man for trespassing. People had heard this, but didn't know what to think. His distant neighbors left him to his own devices.

Next day, the Tindals said that, from the shadows, a friend of theirs had seen the farmer slide his gun out of its holster on the car seat. They told me I was lucky, that he most likely would have shot me if I'd been alone.

The Tindals had invited me to stay with them in the converted pigsty on Jones's property while they harvested his corn. They were his tenants, and I was their guest. But he must have heard I was documenting their life and didn't want a photographer in there taking pictures of this family in such wretched habitation, one of the worst migrant labor camps I'd ever seen. Jones had provided none of the required facilities: there was no running water, no showers, and no toilets. He had taken a structure that once housed pigs, run an underground extension cord from a utility pole to light the bare bulbs on the wood beams of the Tindals' room, and modified it with raised flooring and beds. The available water had to be coaxed from the ground through an old pump that stood in the middle of the yard, the kind of pump that you grab with both hands and pull up and down. The toilet was a walk of about two hundred yards to the woods, a decrepit two-holer outhouse, crawling with bugs and insects.

Later that week, I paid a visit to the Hendersonville migrant clinic and happened to mention this incident to one of the nurses. She said oh, yes, she knew of farmer Jones and in the past had once had quite a run-in with him herself. She said that one of Jones's pickers had met with a serious accident in the orchards, had been disabled, and was found lying under a tree after he had been missing for two days. The clinic was informed and sent its staff out to Jones's farm to fetch the migrant. When they got there, Jones stopped them at his road.

The clinic told the sheriff. He and his deputies escorted the nurses out to the farm and told Jones to step aside, informing him that he would have to let the nurses on his property to bring out the wounded man.

The local authorities said they knew about this labor camp and had tried to close it down five years before. They had told Jones they would bulldoze it if he didn't make it fit for human habitation. Jones had then simply thrown the migrants out and shut it up without making any improvements. When the next season came around, he opened it up again in the same condition.

Last thing I heard about Jones was that he'd choked to death on a chunk of tangerine. "He deserved every bit of it," said L. H. "It didn't come none too soon." What became of his labor camp, I don't know. The Tindals say it's still open.

(1983)

One Day at a Time

L. H.: We are human beings. We're no dogs. We are American-born people. Treat us like Americans. Like we're supposed to be treated, all the way, honestly.

They don't know what a fruit picker is. They just don't know. They don't realize, they just don't dammit understand. We are human beings, just like the rest of the people in this world is. Believe me. They treat me like I was a damn dog. I can't stand it. I'd just like to get down and tell 'em all the way I felt. I just wish they'd let me get on national TV and tell the whole world the way I felt about migrant workers. The way I feel, I get mad when I say it. They treat us like the dogs, like we ain't nothin' but a dog walking on the street. I would tell 'em the way that the migrant workers lived, and the way they low-grade us.

Linda: It's a lot like this . . . you go into a grocery store . . . I took my kids in, just to buy groceries, and the woman said, "Don't you ever give your younguns a bath?" I said, "Lady, have you ever picked oranges before, for a livin'?" A millionaire woman in Loxahatchee, Florida. I said, "Lady," I said, "You have never picked fruit for a living, and wish you hadn't." She didn't have to, but I do.

L. H.: You come into the store, you know what they say? "Look at that trash-ass son of a bitch, look at that nasty bastard. Don't get close to him." You know how she hands your change back? She drops it in your hand. She won't put in in your hand like you're dressed up. You ain't good enough to let her hand touch your hand.

Linda: You leave the field and you go to a grocery store, and somebody jumps on your case for not givin' 'em a bath, and you just left the field. You ain't got a chance to give 'em a bath, no place to give 'em a bath at.

L. H.: Yeah, there's canals. You can give 'em one in a goddamn canal.

Linda: You got to raise 'em the best you can, on a river bank, a creek bank, you got to do your best. Both 'a mine been raised that way. My youngun lived in a tent when he was born. He was born in a tent, the onliest place we had to live. If welfare ever comes in on us and finds out the way we livin' and the way we're raisin' our younguns, you know what it's gonna be? They'll snatch 'em out from under us on account of livin' the way we do.

L. H.: Not livin' the way we do. We livin' the way we *have* to.

Linda: That's the onliest way we can live. We was born, we was raised that way. I was brought up the way the rest of us is. My younguns is brought up into it.

L. H.: What chance you ever get in this life? *None!*

Linda: None in the world. Give us our chance to live. We raised our younguns in canals, raised 'em in an old dump. That's the onliest chance we've got. That's it.

L. H.: It costs us five hunnert dollars a month to even survive. I mean, that's hard. You might work one day, and then it rains six, seven days at a time. What's you gonna do? You gotta bust your can . . .

Linda: You gotta bust your ass to make a livin' while you can, one day at a time.

L. H. lit up. The first puff stung his eyes and he brushed it away. He passed the Bic to Linda just as she was striking a match, one of those red-tipped wooden Diamonds you can ignite anywhere. She pulled it up fast along the leather sole of her boot and put it to her cigarette. Smoke streamed out of her nostrils as she spoke.

Linda: People deprive us of our work, they deprive us of our food and things, people that's got money, they deprive the poor people of it.

L. H.: They can stay in their big fancy hotels, stay in their god-damn big apartments, their hotels, their motels, they got plenty of money. What do we got? We got a beer, right?

Linda: If somebody had a chance, if migrant workers had a chance to get on national TV and tell the rest of 'em what they think, mebbe the world would change.

L. H.: Not the world, the economy.

Linda: We make a per diem. That ain't much.

L. H.: The growers are the same way. You know, like they grow these apples, and like they grow them oranges down yonder, and grapefruit and all? They don't give a damn about us.

Linda: That's right, none of them do, none of them do.

L. H.: They're never 'dere, they don't care, as long as they bring in the almighty dollar to line their pocket.

Linda: As long as they get their money to put in their pocket, damn the fruit pickers.

L. H.: The onliest thing I care about is my kids, that's all I really care about.

Linda: That's the only thing that matters in our life.

L. H.: I don't care about her or I, 'cause we can make it. We're grownups, right? I'm thirty-nine, she's twenty-seven. It's been hard, but I've made it.

Linda: They belong to us . . .

L. H.: Let me re-a-state that. I didn't make it, *we* made it. She and I.

Linda: We made it.

L. H.: Not only me. Hey, I didn't do this on my own. I have been so sick, *not* from drinkin', I have been so sick I couldn't get out of bed.

Linda: I have worked by butt off to make sure they had something to eat when he's sick, laying in the bed, and can't work.

L. H.: I mean, I have been so sick I couldn't get out, but I wouldn't go to the doctor . . .

Linda: I guess it takes two of you. One can't do it alone. It takes two of you pullin'.

L. H.: I swear alive I love my children, and *you,* Linda, more than anythin' in this world.*

(1983)

*Transcript, with permission, from the video production *Fruit Tramps, American Life on the Edge,* by Arthur Kamell, Producer, Director, Editor; Herman Emmet, Still Photography; Dieter Froese, Video Photography; Dekart Video, Production Studios; Copyright, 1983, Witness Films, New York, N.Y.

Linda

Linda, would you mind if I asked you some personal questions over the phone about your life?

No, go right ahead.

At this point, where would you call home?

Wherever I lay my head. Hard to say, wherever we try to head to.

Where do you live now?

We sleep on the beach on Lake Ontario in Olcott, New York, and build a fire to keep warm. When it rains, we sleep under a park picnic table. Have to. We got money, but no one'll rent us a room.

How far have you traveled and what kinds of work have you done?

Michigan for cherries; Ohio for strawberries; Missouri and Mississippi for cotton. That was in the 1960s. The cotton's machine-harvested now; Kentucky for cherries; Texas for public jobs in motels, restaurants, working as a maid, and construction jobs; South Carolina for tomatoes, cucumbers, beans, and such; North Carolina for apples, squash, beans; Georgia for peaches; New York for apples, pears, cherries, cabbage; and Florida for citrus.

What was the citrus piece rate where you picked last winter in Florida?

Sixty cents per box (bushel), which means we got $6 a bin (ten boxes). In upstate New York, we'll pick cherries 'til September, 'til the apples come in. In cherries, we'll make about $1.75 per lug (one-half bushel). We pick with a basket tied around the waist.

What season has no citrus jobs in Florida?

The midseason, the last of July through October. The citrus season runs roughly from November through July depending, 'a course, on the weather; the freezes, the rains, the droughts, and such.

Have you and L. H. done nonagricultural jobs during the midseason, or during slack times, to tide you over?

Yes, we have: things like auto mechanic, front-end man, brick mason, house painter, laying shingles, housing construction, public jobs, maid.

How much do you two make in a year?
$2,000 to $3,000 in a good year. This year L. H. made $784.05, and I made $526.02.

How much education do you have?

I only went through to the tenth grade, Lincoln Park High, Ft. Pierce, Florida. L. H. done the same. Dropped out at the tenth grade, Lexington High, Lexington, South Carolina.

How long have you and L. H. known each other, and how did you two meet?

Through my daddy Leroy. L. H. worked for Leroy picking citrus. Leroy was a crew chief. L. H. also worked for him as a tractor mechanic. We met when I was thirteen. L. H. was twenty-five. 'Bout fifteen years ago. 1969. He bounced me on his knee. Swore one day he'd marry me. He did.

What did your families do before you and L. H.?

Fruit pickers all their life. My granddaddy James and my momma's daddy worked cotton. L. H.'s daddy Woodrow traveled all over picking cotton and fruit. L. H.'s momma's daddy Sonny was a full-blooded Indian, a Cherokee.

What kind of future do you see for your children, Tina Michelle
and Shannon DeWayne?

They'll grow up to be fruit pickers like us.

(1984)

Too Thin for Snow

L. H. may not have a thing to show for his crazy fruit-tramp life, but says he'd never change it for anything in the world. He's a free man and chose this migrant life. If he had a million dollars, he says, he'd still wear the same raggedy clothes. Made more money than most men see in a lifetime, never saved a dime of it. Says he'd rather give it away than save it.

Swears that he wants to settle down for his children's sake, for them to get an education. "I only give a damn for my kids and my wife," L. H. says. "I love my family. It's all I need. It's all I got." But he would have to give up his migrant ways.

In 1984, the Tindals went to Olcott Beach on Lake Ontario in western New York State to do apples. There, they put Tina and Shannon in school, and rented a second-story apartment, above a bar with pool tables and a strip joint. At night, you could hear the wild music and cat calls from below, and fist fights in the street. "But," said Linda, "Jackie, the owner, was the only one in Olcott to take us in. No one else would 'cause we looked like bums on account 'a having to live in the park like animals."

"You know," said L. H., "when we first came into town, we went right over 'dere to that motel, the one up near the marina and them fancy boats. But the man wouldn't rent us a room, no sir. Said he had no vacancy. I said, Well how come you got your vacancy sign on outside and 'dere ain't but two cars at your motel? He said, That's what I said, and I mean it. And I said, Well, you can take your motel and shove it.

That was that, and, of course, the Tindals are not the easiest people to deal with. They don't beat around the bush. They'll let you know if you're giving them the short end of the stick, or staring at them because of the way they look: poor, blown out, and on the wild side. Once, in an Italian restaurant outside Olcott, near Newfane, we were all diving into our spaghetti when L. H. yelled across the room, "Well, what are you looking at, fatso?" The beefy man with his family turned crimson, his wife glared at us from the corner of her eyes, his kids cringed.

But once set up in Olcott, the Tindals started feeling good about themselves. They weren't exactly flush, but apple money was good, twice as good as it was down South. "We done hung up our travelin' shoes, and we're staying put," Linda said over the phone. "Yep, Olcott's the end of the line for us. When are you comin' to visit?"

I did. Went to the orchards, met their new friends, played pool, watched the fleshy bare stripper bump and grind, arm-wrestled with L. H., horsed with Tina as she did cartwheels on the beach, took pictures of Shannon Dewayne in his new Sunday seersucker suit. I saw the sparkle in their eyes. They drove me around, showed me their new final stop. They'd tried before, but'd never quit running. They reassured me. "This is it. We're gettin' too old to keep up the travelin'. And besides," said L. H., grinning, "these Yankees ain't half so bad."

They left the crummy strip-joint apartment for a real house around the corner on Main Street, rent-free in exchange for sweat-equity repair work. They even put in a phone. "Now we can call Mamma and not have to drag the kids to some filthy phone booth,' said Linda. "It feels like home." It was a turning point.

I visited again in the fall of 1985 and took pictures for an *Esquire* photo essay to appear in the spring of 1986. And because Linda and L. H. had chosen to settle down for good, the piece was called "The End of the Road." A more sanguine couple never existed. "It's one thing to quit roamin', it's another to read about it. 'Though I can't say I'd mind. It'll be a pleasure when it comes out. Hell, what we been through together, Herman, you, me, Linda, and the kids, it's about time."

At dusk, L. H. and I went for a walk on the beach that was once their home. A raw October wind blew across the lake from Canada, pushing the dark water up the sand to touch our shoes. Only the outline of his weatherbeaten face and his open red flannel shirt and flapping tails were visible, chest bared to the soughing gusts as we bumped arms. "You treat me like a man, Herman, not like a dog," he said. "That's why I'll always be your friend."

Then they disappeared. Gone. Not a trace. Called up one of the old farmers they'd picked for, but he hadn't seen them since the snows. Jackie at the Olcotta Bar hadn't seen them since the weather'd turned cold. That was my clue. They'd always said their blood was like their shoes: too thin for snow.

In the spring of 1986, Linda called from a public phone booth in Florida. "We got your letter the other day wondrin' where we'd gone to. Well, we're in Wahneta, on 5th Street East, trailer number 26, an' been doin' citrus over near Orlando. We just got tired of the snow and the cold in Olcott. Couldn't hack it. Besides, we ain't got the right clothes for that kind 'a climate. Plus the cops was somethin' else. Told us to get out or they'd lock us up. But, anyway, I wanna tell you what just happened."

Inside a Seven Eleven, a cashier had asked her if she was a fruit picker. "Sure am," Linda replied. Well, the woman said, she had just seen a magazine story with pictures and all about a migrant family and, that she, Linda, should read it, because it was all about her own kind. "As a matter of fact," said the cashier, "you kinda look like the woman in the pictures." Linda ran out of the store.

Linda felt shy, but proud. After all these years, it had finally happened. The story was out. Bull's eye. This was all too real. Quick, tell L. H. and the kids.

(1984–86)

Clots

October 27

Doctor had to take her from me with a suction cup . . . caused blood clots on her brain . . . had the navel cord hooked around her neck . . . had surgery in a West Palm Beach hospital for a hole in her heart and kidney disease . . . now she's on a heart machine and I.V.'s . . . born 6 lbs. 10 oz. . . . name's Nikki Nicole . . . said Linda.

(1986)

TB

May 1

Linda called collect yesterday from Fort Pierce, Florida, said L. H. was dying from tuberculosis, was in a semiconscious state, could not speak because of throat cancer, and probably would not live much longer. "They come and took L. H. away, to a sanitarium where I cain't see him," she said, crying softly. "I'm alone, no job, no money, and nary a speck o' food for my kids."

Went out looking for a job, she said, "but no one'll hire me. Haf to go on welfare to survive." I told her I was truly sorry, to keep in touch, and wired her $200.

August 19

L. H. got up and walked out of the sanitarium because he'd had enough, and took the family back to South Carolina. "If I'm going to die, let me die where I was born." Eventually Linda prevailed, and sent L. H. back to Florida where he underwent successful surgery to remove a cancerous throat tumor. They think the TB is cured, or at least manageable. But they're not sure, not even about the cancer.

They're staying with friends near Pelion, S.C., 'til they figure out what to do next. As there are no crops to pick in the area, they're "layin' low, takin' one day at a time."

(1987)

Pelion

During a humid spring visit of mine to the Tindals, beautiful thir-teen-year-old Tina Michelle turns and says, "Hey, Herman, take me to Lexington, to go shopping, just the two of us." I've known her since she was three. I oblige. It's hot as we ride into town, and I turn on the air. She fiddles with the radio and finds some country. I ask her how things are going at school. Says fine, then tells me that when she grows up, wants to be a math and English teacher because she likes those subjects a lot, and because she loves her teacher, Miss Beth Edens, who has taught her everything at the Pelion Elementary School since Christmas.

We stop at Hardee's for lunch. If she'd been with her parents in the rusty, faded Buick, old clothes, six bare feet and mother's pregnant belly, people would've looked and whispered behind their coffee cups. Instead, they see her pull in an '88 shiny rental, with new shoes and an average-looking, middle-class man, and probably think, isn't that nice, father taking daughter out for a Saturday treat. Tina orders a hamburger, fries, and a coke.

In between slurps on the straw, she says there are about thirty kids in her one class with Miss Edens, but that next school year she'll have a different teacher in every subject. She'll be in sixth grade then, a year behind the others because of migrant life. I ask her if that makes her feel different from the other kids. Says, no, it don't.

> *I live in a regular house, ain't like rich people with millions of dollars who live in these nice brick homes. I'd rather not like to be a rich person. I like livin' the way I am. I'm proud the way I live and the way I am. I like wearin' my old faded jeans with the holes in them. People say in the grocery stores, "I don't understand how y'all live like that." If they don't like the way we're livin', they should buy us things. They can always turn their heads and not look.*

Outside, behind the small rented Tindal trailer, Tina Michelle plays with Shannon Dewayne, their seven cousins, and five next-door trailer kids. Inside, in the hot bedroom where soft country plays twenty-four hours with stereo light-emitting diodes pulsing on the sides of a boom-box radio, L. H. rests up sick from a troubled night. At the kitchen table, near a rusted-out stove one of whose burners out of four works, and a teetering ice-box whose door is propped shut with the back of a chair whose cane seat has collapsed into a tattered hole, Linda and I compare notes about how Tina is looking very grown-up, and about the local school situation. Tina may say she doesn't feel very different from some of her classmates, but she does, says Linda, and it's not just her torn clothes. Other kids dress neat, have money for new things, and, yes, some are rich. But it's not so much what they are, as what they say.

The kids in school talk about the way we live, places we live in, how dirty and nasty they are. It hurts Tina's feelings, bothers her. Tina tells 'em, "you ain't got to live it." It makes her angry and she fights them. Causes it to get her in trouble in school. She beats 'em up. Tina and the other migrant kids feel like outsiders.

Linda's tee shirt swells from the baby inside her; Christine Angelica. She knows it's a girl. Shows me the sonogram picture of her fetus. She shifts in her chair to get comfortable and, lying back, slides her feet straight out. Says her past pregnancies were never this bad. Takes medication for the pain. Reaches into her faded jeans with stringy cuffs, pulls out a round container, pops the lid, and washes down two pills with a swallow of Diet Coke.

Thinks Tina will probably fit in more at school as time goes by. She's already a B student, and despite some snide things kids say in the classroom, has lots of school friends, especially her cousins, and kids of farmer and farmworker families who work in the fields. Tina has a good, loving home life, Linda feels, never complains, likes to go swimming a lot, and wants to grow up like her daddy and be a fruit tramp.

I think a lot of young kids would like to know the life I grew up in, and that Tina grew up in. There's nothin' the matter with it. They think we shouldn't be brought up this way. They could learn how difficult it is to make it in migrant life. I am happy with my life.

A couple of days later, while remembering these two separate conversations, I ask Tina how she can be a teacher *and* a fruit tramp. Says she knows it would take a long time to be a good teacher, and that it would be hard work, but she could do both if she really tried.

I like my parents and their life. I'd like to follow in my momma's and daddy's footprints. I'm proud of their footprints, who they are. People should know about type of life we lead, where the fruit comes from. The most fun time I ever had was in the grove, just being around my parents and pickin' fruit, all the traveling, new places all the time. I never wished I had another family.

While L. H. and I are shooting pool of an afternoon at his sister's wooden convenience store, Linda drives up to their wretched trailer and catches the landlord ripping out the water spigot from her yard. She and L. H. grow beans, lettuce, peas, okra, and the like there, and need water. All their migrant life they've wanted a garden. "Feels more like home," says Linda. She moves toward the landlord, and he backs down the slope to his house across the street. He's Will O'Borne, and they call him a mail-order bride.

People say that his wife got him through a catalogue, and that he came to rural South Carolina from the New York Catskill mountains, a Yankee outsider. He is a good cook, L. H. concedes, but a "meaner, stupider, sonovabitch never existed." Ray, whom I met at Kirklands' grocery store while drinking beer, says O'Borne must be half-crazy, making a habit of renting out trailers and then, within a few weeks, running out his tenants. Doesn't see how a man like that can do business, let alone make money.

If you got no family in this life, says L. H., you ain't got nothin'. Like, I'm blind in one eye. I get three-forty-one a month in social security for disability. Linda gets a hunnert and ninety-three a month in food stamps. That's a total of five hunnert and thirty-four dollars between us. After we pay the utilities and rent to that sonovabitch Yankee landlord across the street for this trailer-dump we live in, we got nary a dime for food. But we got credit at the Kirklands' store. We pay off the markers and they give us credit. Why? 'Cause we're kin, me and the Kirklands, like most everybody around here is. If yo' kin don't help you out, who will?

L. H. gets home, takes one look at the capped pipe and shoots down the hill in long strides to the edge of the road. Linda yells, "Git back in here, L. H." She is afraid for him, not for what he might do, but because he might get shot.

He is careful not to trespass, just the kind of move a man like O'Borne is waiting for. So he stands in the middle of the road with his legs wide apart, fists clenched at the sky, and with his fine mouth, villifies the landlord. Neighbors stop, stare and listen.

He challenges O'Borne to a fight, to come out like a man, not like a mail-order bride. The landlord mumbles from the veranda that he'll call the cops if he keeps this up. L. H. says, go ahead, call the cops, see if I give a damn, I ain't got nothing to lose. I'll tell 'em what you done to me and my family; you shot my dog, you snuck onto my place, and took away my water.

The neighbors witnessed the puppy's death, they say. O'Borne claimed it was bothering his billygoat. One day he took out his firearm and destroyed the dog, a Christmas gift from L. H. and Linda to their children, a cuddly black mutt. One thing for sure, says Linda, it musta been the only pup in creation that ever messed with a nasty, full-grown billygoat. A few weeks later, O'Borne got them evicted from his trailer through a local judge.

These rich people around here, they like to keep us down, down under their feet. Know what I mean? They think they're better'n us, remarks L. H., like that man Louche, the one you met up at the Kirkland's store. Me and my daddy used to pick his cotton, and I used to plow his mule, 'bout thirty years ago. But he thinks he's better'n me and my kind, the poor people.

56

Hell, I put my trousers on the same way he puts his on. Ain't no difference.

Workers in local government agencies are sometimes just a notch above the Tindals and hate their guts. They see poor white trash coming through the door and put on serious faces and cross their arms and say there's no money. One of Linda's sisters, pregnant and needing help, was denied food stamps. She asked the white woman clerk across the desk whether she'd stand a better chance of getting food stamps if she tarred her face. The woman said, yes, she would.

In Aiken (S.C.), we went to apply for food stamps. They told us we wasn't qualified, relates L. H., 'cause we wasn't making a hunnert dollars a week. They turned us flat down. So we went to see Senator Strom Thurmond at his headquarters down in Aiken, talked with his secretary. She got on the computer to Washington, and a week later we got a little over eight-hunnert dollars in food stamps. I don't know how they was able to do it. But they told us they'd close the food stamp office down if they refused us any assistance. The food stamp office sent us a letter to come see them. We got a letter from the senator, too. The bullshit 'bout makin' a hunnert dollars a week is just that. Bullshit!

The social worker in Aiken told the landlord to have me and my family evicted 'cause I had T.B. So I went back to the senator's office, and they sent a letter to the landlord saying that my T.B. was noncommunicable, and that if the landlord tried to evict me, still tried to mess around with me, I would end up ownin' the place. The social worker lost her job. As long as I'm on medication, my T.B. is noncommunicable. The nurse comes out here Tuesdays and Fridays, brings me Rifadin, Vitamin B6, and some other drug.

One day out of the blue, L. H. asks, "Why are you down here this time, Herman?" "I'm here because you're dying, and I wanted to see you before, you know, before you died."

This last private moment we had, May 26, 1988, we rode down the narrow country highway reminiscing, philosophizing, trying out our individual thoughts and feelings on each other. L. H. was not looking well. Too thin, I thought. But he still had plenty of spunk. Said one of his sisters had the eye out for me, that I sure had a lot of talent with the ladies. Told him he didn't do too badly, himself, in that department. We laughed. I wondered to myself if it *would* be our last time. Turned the rental onto a red clay road that would take us a mile or so down to a friend's house. L. H. had come to collect on a loan.

Luther Henry is a rural personality. A holdover from the old South, he is a rebel at heart and in his mind.

I got throat cancer and t.b. The doctor said, Mr. Tindal, you're gonna die soon. But that was last year and I'm still livin'. Linda won't let me out of her sight. She knows I could go any time. If I have to die, lemme go home and die, back where my roots is. I ain't afraid to die. I'm ready to go. I just don't like staying dead so long. I want to come back to see how the rest of the world's doin'. I wanna see my ole friens.

All my family's been comin' round 'cause they know. Most of them I don't like, but I done made my peace. If one of my family wants to commit suicide, I'll stand right dere and say, go ahead, pull the trigger, be a damn fool. But me, I'm gonna go on livin'. I love life.

(May 1988)

Carolina 1979

L. H. Tindal climbing wooden ladder to pick apples, near Saluda, South Carolina.
Permanent collection, Museum of Modern Art, New York.

Linda Inez Tindal, carrying ladder to tree to pick apples, with pick sack around waist.
Edneyville, North Carolina.

L. H. pushing apple bin, carrying pick sack,
Rutherfordton, North Carolina.

L. H., Linda, and Tina Michelle picking apples,
near Dana, North Carolina.

Tina climbing in apple bin to remove leaves and twigs from apples while parents
pick nearby, Dana, North Carolina.

Tina eating apples for lunch, Dana, North Carolina.

Calvin Tindal harvesting squash, Dana, North Carolina.

"Monkey" (Luther Henry, Jr.) Tindal harvesting squash, Dana, North Carolina.

Calvin, Lewis, and L. H. Tindal harvesting squash,
Dana, North Carolina.

Tina in bean field, Edneyville, North Carolina.

Monkey and Tina harvesting beans, Edneyville, North Carolina.

Tina (running) and L. H. (walking under laundry) outside their house on
Hogrock Road, Edneyville, North Carolina.

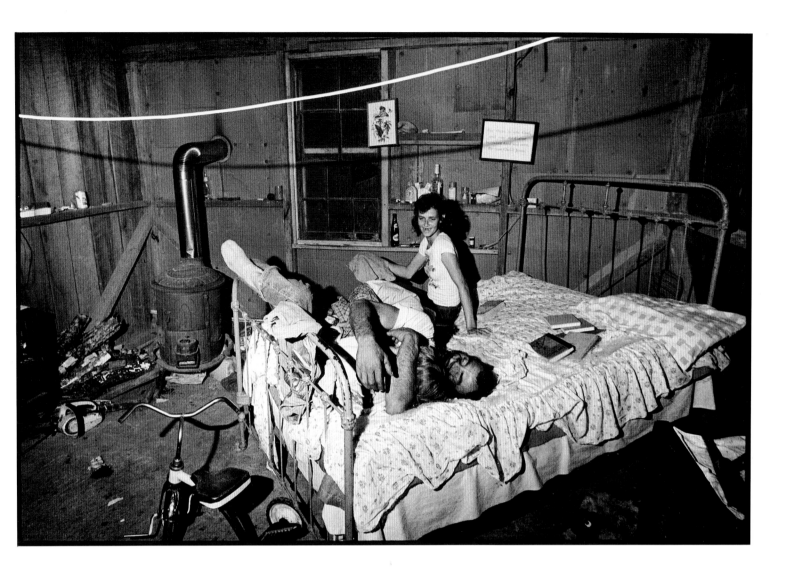

Linda, L. H., and Tina, Edneyville, North Carolina.

Tina warming her feet at oven, sitting on empty herbicide bucket,
Edneyville, North Carolina.

L. H. and Linda, gambling, Edneyville, North Carolina.

L. H. serving himself lima beans with pork, Hogrock Road,
Edneyville, North Carolina.

Linda handling money during poker game, Edneyville, North Carolina.

L. H. exiting converted school bus toilet/shower in migrant labor camp,
Edneyville, North Carolina.

Linda, Calvin, Tina, and L. H. Tindal in converted school bus,
Edneyville, North Carolina.

Tina, Linda, and L. H. taking break from picking,
Rutherfordton, North Carolina.

Woodrow Tindal (L. H.'s father) holding granddaughter,
Edneyville, North Carolina.

L. H. Tindal, Edneyville, North Carolina.

Woodrow Tindal, Edneyville, North Carolina.

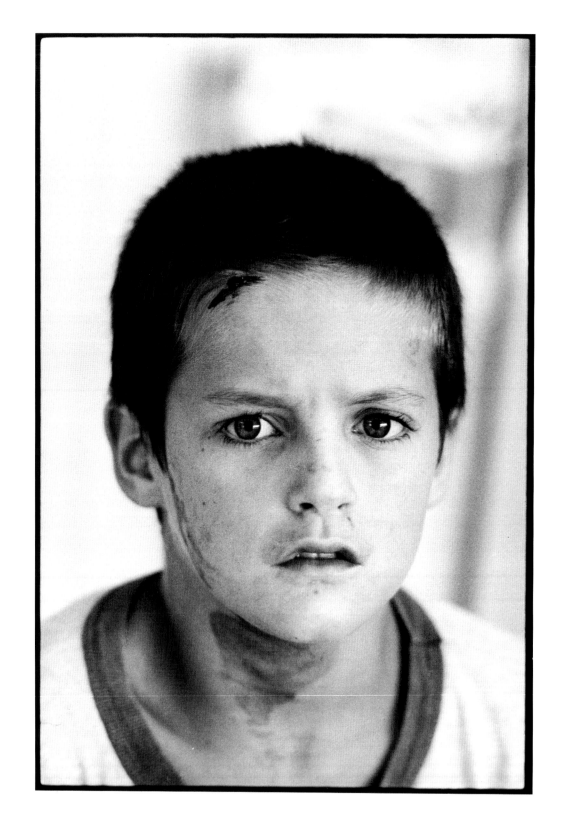

Monkey after hitting his head on a boulder while picking,
Hendersonville, North Carolina.

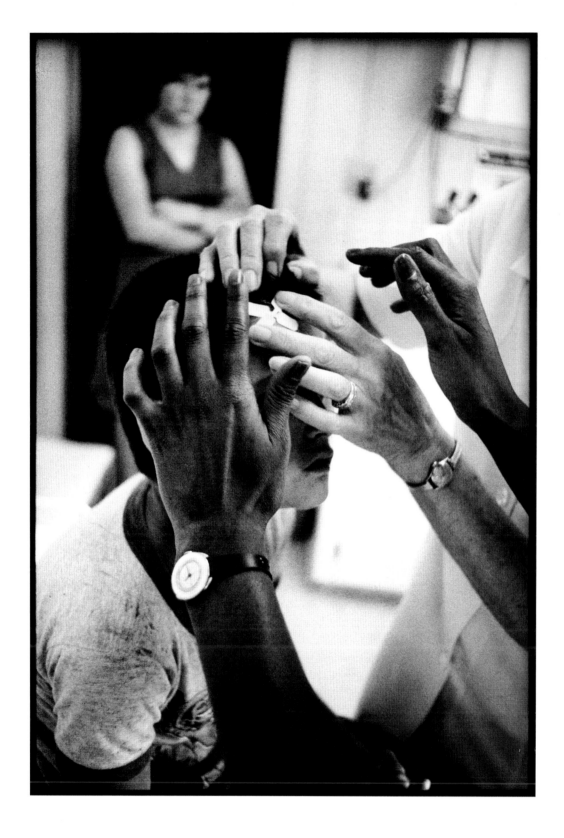

Monkey being patched up at Hendersonville Migrant Clinic,
Hendersonville, North Carolina.

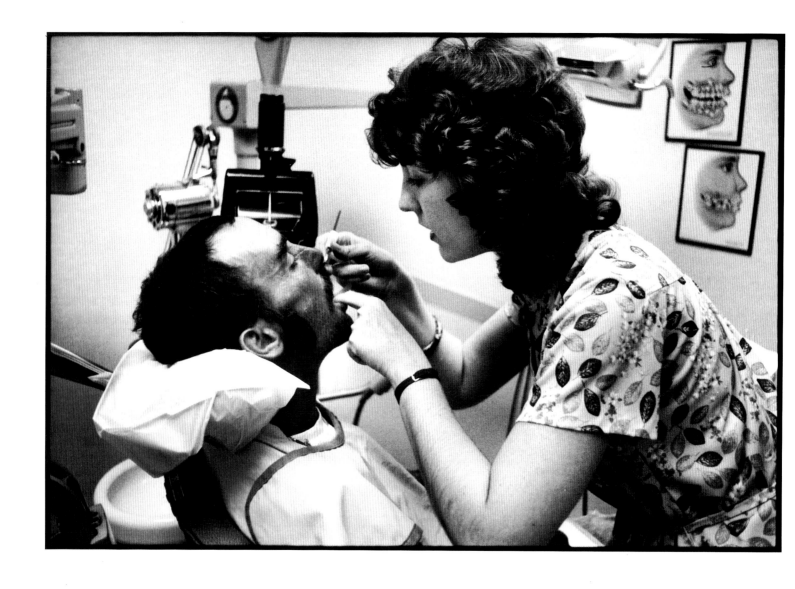

L. H. Tindal being examined at dentist's office, Hendersonville, North Carolina.

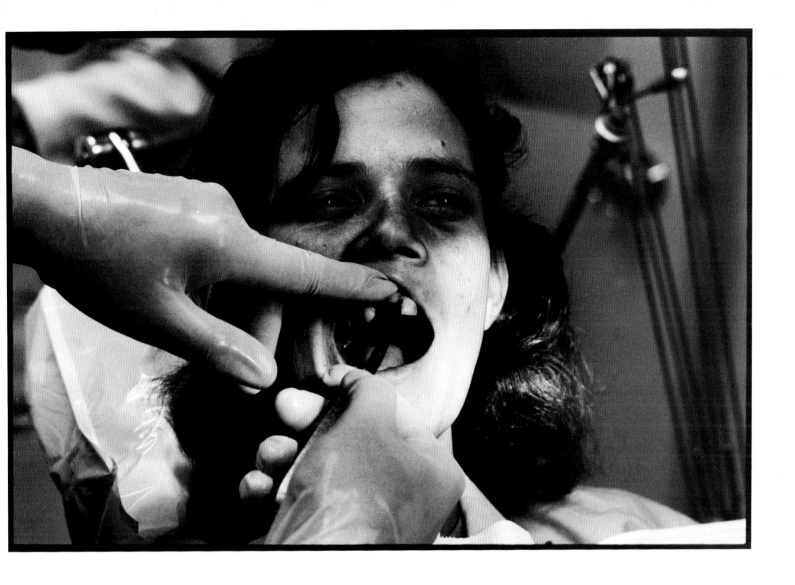

Linda having teeth extracted, Hendersonville, North Carolina.

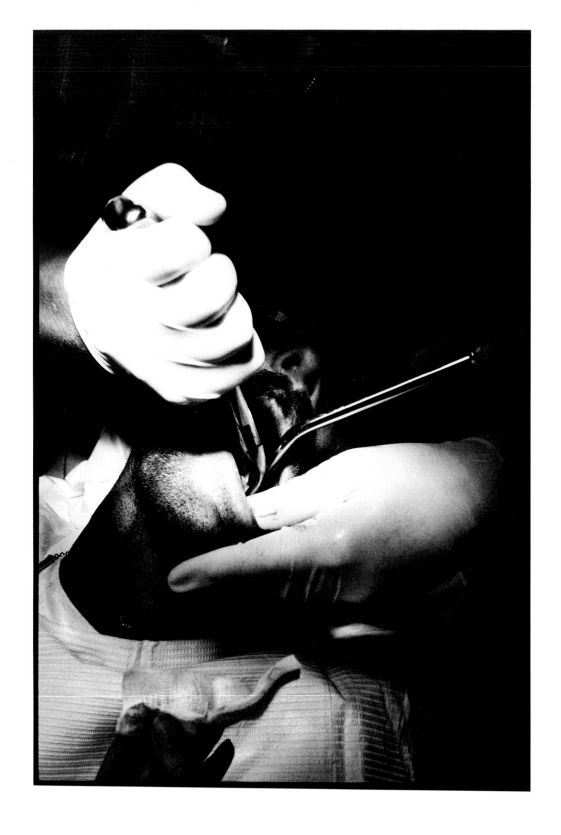

L. H. having teeth extracted, Hendersonville, North Carolina.

Florida 1981

L. H. carrying son, Shannon Dewayne, Loxahatchee, Florida.

Linda cooking and Tina watching campfire near family tent in citrus grove on the
edge of the Everglades, Loxahatchee, Florida

L. H. holding onto Tina's legs, with Shannon and Linda eating jack mackerel stew.
Note tattoos on L. H.'s shoulders and chest: "Live hard, love fast, die young."

Calvin Tindal and friend Ray foraging for firewood near Loxahatchee.

L. H. foraging for firewood near Loxahatchee.

L. H. and Calvin Tindal carrying firewood on the hood of L. H.'s Dodge Dart,
Loxahatchee, Florida.

Tindal family camp in citrus grove, Loxahatchee, Florida.

Tina walking on levee while Linda washes hair in citrus irrigation canal,
Loxahatchee, Florida.

Tina bathing in irrigation canal, Loxahatchee, Florida.

Linda bathing Shannon in irrigation canal, Loxahatchee, Florida.

Linda with Shannon and Tina, Loxahatchee, Florida.

Calvin Tindal emptying citrus pick sack while Shannon watches oranges fall into
plastic tub, Loxahatchee, Florida.

Linda lowering fruit ladder to Calvin.

The Tindals taking a break, near St. Lucie Locks, Florida.

The Tindals taking a break under Tropicana truck,
near St. Lucie Locks, Florida.

Linda shopping with Tina and Shannon, Wellington, Florida.

L. H. shopping for heavy picking gloves, convenience store,
Loxahatchee, Florida.

Shannon and Tina, St. Lucie Locks, Florida.

Carolina 1981

L. H. visiting site of homestead where he grew up, Guinea Swamp,
near Pelion, South Carolina.

Linda cutting through woods with Shannon followed by other family members and
friends, near Chimney Rock, North Carolina.
Permanent collection, Museum of Modern Art, New York.

Linda and Shannon bathing in creek near Chimney Rock, North Carolina.

Tina watching poker game, Dana, North Carolina.

Tina working pump, Dana, North Carolina.

Tina bathing in sink in converted school bus, Edneyville, North Carolina.

Linda taking Tina to school bus, Edneyville, North Carolina.

Lake Ontario, New York State
and Florida 1984–1986

L. H. and Linda, Olcott, New York, 1984.

The Tindals in public park, Olcott, New York, 1984. They lived on the beach and slept under the table when it rained.

Tina walking toward family on jetty into Lake Ontario, Olcott, New York, 1984.

Linda and L. H. cutting cabbage, near Appleton, New York, 1985.

Linda and L. H. posing in Olcott before heading out to pick apples
near Newfane, New York, 1985.

L. H. and Linda taking break from "grove work" (cleaning dead brush, pruning trees, etc.), near Ft. Pierce, Florida, 1986.

L. H. wielding machete, doing grove work, near Ft. Pierce, Florida, 1986.

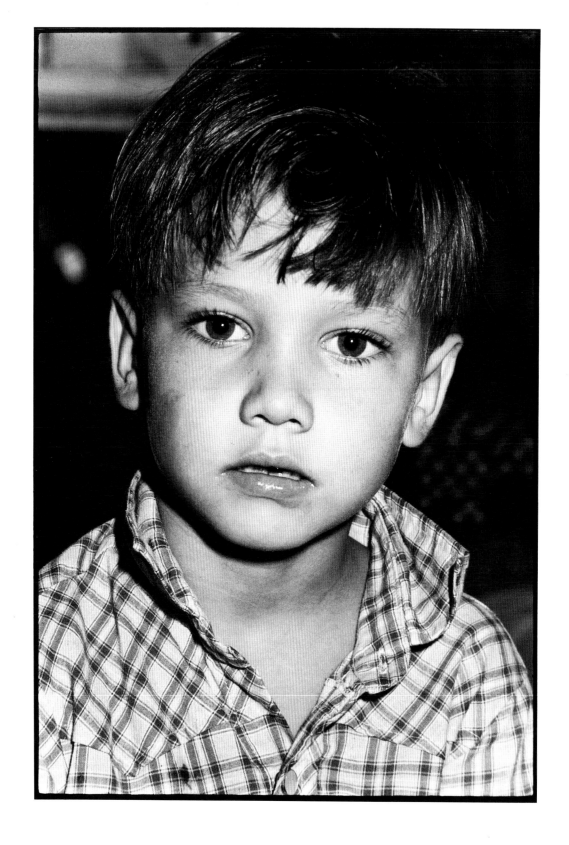

Shannon Dewayne Tindal, 1986.

Shannon dressed for his first Halloween party, Olcott, New York, 1985.

Tina Michelle Tindal, 1986.

Tina dressed for her first Halloween party, Olcott, New York, 1985.

Luther Henry Tindal, 1985.

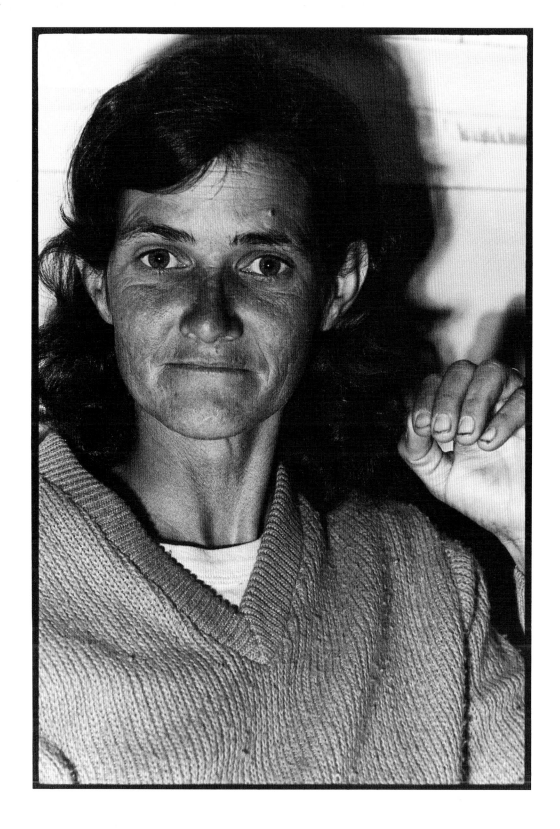

Linda Inez Tindal, 1985.

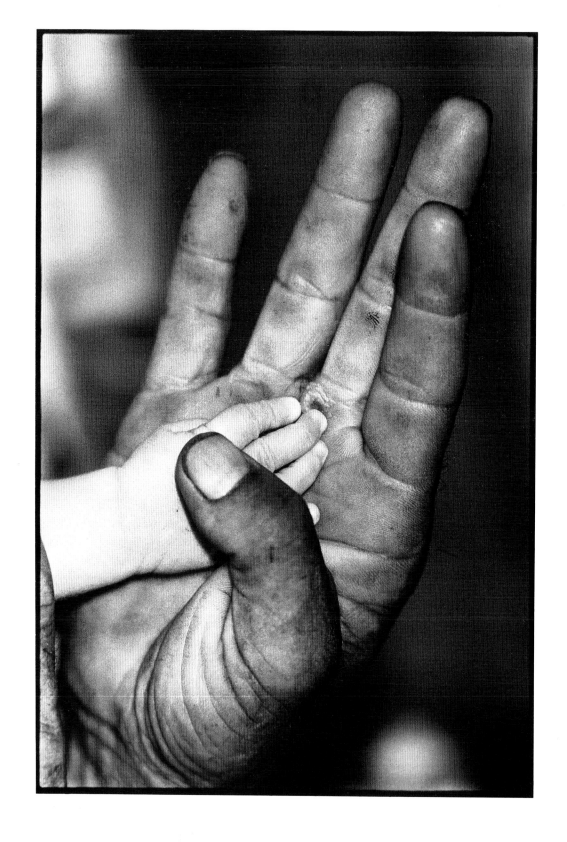

Right hand of Nikki Nicole Tindal (about two weeks old)
held by L. H.'s right hand, 1986.

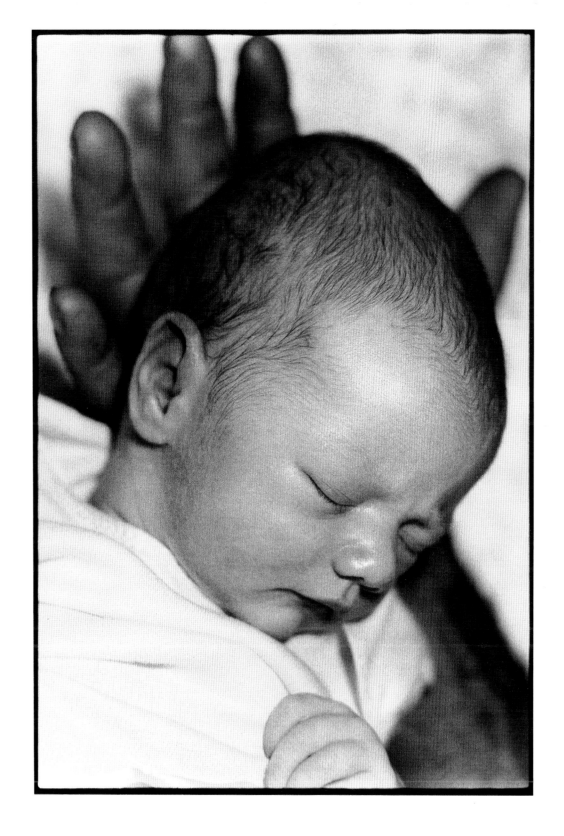

Nikki Nicole Tindal, 1986.

Shannon and Tina beside family trailer, Ft. Pierce, Florida, 1986.

Tindal family in trailer, Ft. Pierce, Florida, 1986.

Design by Milenda Nan Ok Lee
Typography in Spartan by the
University of New Mexico Printing Services
Printed in a first edition of 500 casebound
and 2000 paperback copies by Dai Nippon Printing Co., Ltd.
Printed in Japan